Metadense Omniangular Polyadaptive Transband Metacell Metaradome

Mori no Prince

Metadense Omniangular Polyadaptive Transband Metacell Metaradome

First Edition November 2025

Written by Mori no Prince

TABLE OF CONTENTS

LIST OF TABLES

LIST OF FIGURES

FIGURE NO.	TITLE	PAGE NO.

LIST OF SYMBOLS AND ABBREVIATIONS

4G	-	4th Generation
5G	-	5th Generation
ADS	-	Advanced Design System
AWS	-	Advanced Wireless Services
AMC	-	Artificial Magnetic Conductor
CPW	-	Coplanar Waveguide
DSRC	-	Dedicated Short-Range Communication
DGS	-	Defected Ground Structure
EBG	-	Electromagnetic Band-Gap
FPRA	-	Fabry-Perot Resonator Antenna
FDTD	-	Finite Difference Time Domain
GPS	-	Global Positioning System
GSM	-	Global System for Mobile
HFSS	-	High Frequency Structure Simulator
Li-Fi	-	Light Fidelity
LTCC	-	Low Temperature Co-fired Ceramics technology
MOM	-	Method of Moment
MEMS	-	Micro-Electro-Mechanical Systems
MICs	-	Microwave integrated circuits
MMW	-	Millimeter Wave
MIMO	-	Multi-Input-Multi-Output

MMR	-	Multi-Mode Resonator
OAM	-	Orbital angular Momentum
PSO	-	Particle Swarm Optimization
PIFA	-	Printed Inverted-F Antenna
RF	-	Radio Frequency
RFID	-	Radio Frequency Identification tag
SPDT	-	Single Pole Double Throw
UWB	-	Ultra-Wide Band
UAV	-	Unmanned Aircraft Vehicle
VNA	-	Vector Network Analyzer
VSWR	-	Voltage Standing Wave Ratio
WRA	-	Waveguide Resonator Antenna
Wi-Fi	-	Wireless Fidelity
WLAN	-	Wireless local Area Network
WiMAX	-	Worldwide Interoperability for Microwave Access

-

CHAPTER 1

INTRODUCTION

1.1 PREAMBLE

Communication is the process by which messages or information are shared between living beings. In the modern era, digital technologies have revolutionized communication, enabling more sophisticated and connected human life. Continuous advancements in these technologies have made communication faster, more reliable, and more efficient through various means. Recent innovations such as Bluetooth, WLAN, WiMAX, 5G Wi-Fi (Wireless Fidelity), and Li-Fi (Light Fidelity) have transformed the way data is transmitted and received. At the core of these technologies lies the antenna — a transducer that converts electrical energy into electromagnetic waves. The design of an antenna involves several engineering approaches aimed at enhancing its performance and, consequently, the overall efficiency of the communication system. Over the years, numerous antenna design methodologies have been proposed, fabricated, and experimentally evaluated to determine their effectiveness. These approaches help in identifying optimal design parameters that maximize performance. This thesis presents a detailed investigation of various microstrip antenna design techniques developed for modern wireless communication systems.

1.2 ANTENNA – AN INTRODUCTION

According to the IEEE standard, an antenna is defined as "a means for radiating or receiving radio waves." It is essentially a physical arrangement of metallic conductors connected electrically to a transmitter or receiver, enabling the conversion between electromagnetic fields and alternating currents. At the transmitting end, alternating currents are driven through the conductors to generate oscillating magnetic fields, which propagate as electromagnetic waves. At the receiving end, these fields induce voltages that can be processed by the receiver.

Antennas that transmit radio frequency signals are known as transmitting antennas, while those that capture such signals are called receiving antennas. They are indispensable components in various communication systems, including radio, wireless local area networks, mobile communication, and satellite systems. The rapid advancements in wireless technologies—such as WLAN, GPS, mobile phones, and Bluetooth—have led to a growing demand for compact and efficient antennas and filters. Integrating both elements into a single, miniaturized module enhances overall system performance by improving filtering and radiation characteristics. To meet modern communication requirements, antennas must exhibit sharp frequency selectivity, good harmonic suppression, and adjustable bandwidth.

Antennas are broadly classified based on their directional characteristics into omnidirectional, directional, and arbitrary types. Omnidirectional antennas radiate and receive signals uniformly in the horizontal plane, whereas directional or high-gain antennas focus energy in specific directions to achieve greater range and efficiency. Parasitic elements and parabolic reflectors are often incorporated to shape the desired radiation pattern. Ultimately, antenna design depends on the intended application—whether for smartphones, cellular networks, GPS systems, or Wi-Fi communication—each requiring tailored structural and electrical characteristics to optimize performance.

1.2.1 Working Principle of Antenna

Microphones convert sound energy into electrical, which is made to flow along a tall metal antenna at the transmitting end. The electrons in the electric current twist back and forth along the antenna and create electromagnetic radiation. This radiation is termed as radio waves. These waves are partly electrical and partly magnetic and travel at speed of light. The radio waves will be received at the receiving end through the metal antenna, which causes the electrons to wiggle and generates electric current signal. This signal is converted back into sound waves. This is the working phenomenon of antenna.

1.3 TYPES OF ANTENNAS

Antennas are classified based on their structure, characteristics and applications. The classification is given as follows:

(i) Based on Structure

- Dipole and Monopole Antenna
- Corner-Reflector Antenna
- Yagi Antenna

(ii) Based on characteristics and applications

- Wire antennas
- Aperture antennas
- Array antennas

- ➢ Reflector antennas
- ➢ Lens antennas
- ➢ Microstrip Antennas

1.3.1 Classification Based on Structure

Antennas are classified based on frequency band of operation, physical structure, electrical / electromagnetic design, directions etc. The most simple and common type of antenna used are non-directional antennas. The se antennas may be monopole or dipole antennas. The complex antenna structure consists of arrays of elements, viz. dipoles, active or passive elements. Yagi antenna is one among the most popular complex antenna structures. Applications decide the type of antenna to be used. Many researchers focus on improving the design of new antenna technologies. These improvements or changes allow antenna to change its pattern rapidly in response to changes in the direction of arrival of the receiving signal. Such type of antennas is termed a "Smart Antennas" and is used for the higher frequency bands. In the following section, the few commonly used antenna structure have been described.

1.3.1.1 Dipole and Monopole Antenna

Dipole antenna is an Omni directional (in azimuth) antenna. When the wavelength of the antenna is equal to half of its original wavelength, then the antenna possess a gain of 1.64 i.e. Gain = 2.15 dBi, in the horizontal plane. Figure 1.1 (a) illustrates a centre-fed, vertical dipole antenna structure. Though this structure is simple, it finds difficult to mount on a mast or a vehicle. The ideal vertical monopole antenna is illustrated in Figure 1.1 (b). The monopole antenna is a half dipole structure placed in half space, with a perfectly conducting, infinite surface at the boundary. The vertical dipole or monopole antenna structure finds most suitable for the Land Mobile Radio System applications.

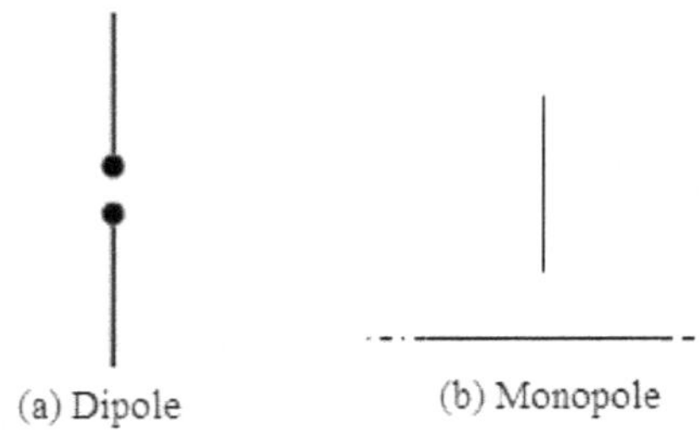

Figure 1.1 Vertical Dipole and Monopole Antenna Structures

A monopole antenna is similar to the dipole antenna, in an infinite ground palne on a free space. The identical monopole antenna has identical gain and pattern similar to dipole in the half-space above the ground plane. Practically, the ground nplane cannot be infinite. It is with a radius approximately the same as the length of the active element. The flat surface on which the antenna is mounted i.e vehicle's trunk or roof will act as an adequate ground pane. Figure 1.2 depicts the tyepical monoploe antennas for base station and mobile applications.

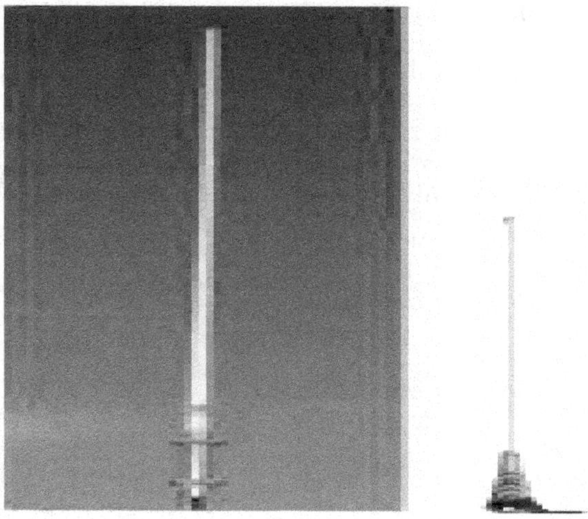

(a) Base-Station Applicaions (b) Mobile Applications

Figure 1.2 Typical Monopole Antennas

1.3.1.2 Corner Reflector

Corner-reflector antenna comprises of one or more dipole elements in front of a corner reflector, as depicted in Figure 1.3.

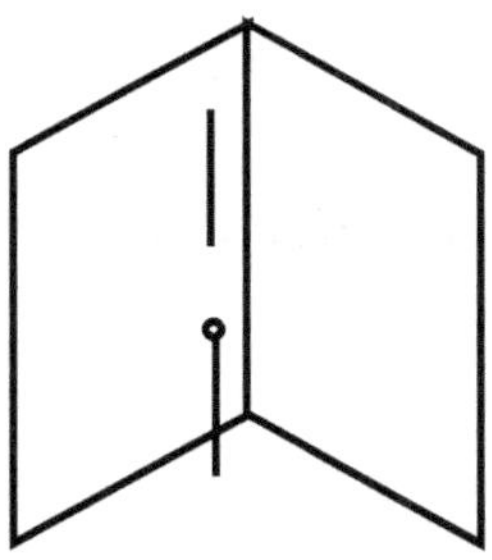

(a) Solid Reflector

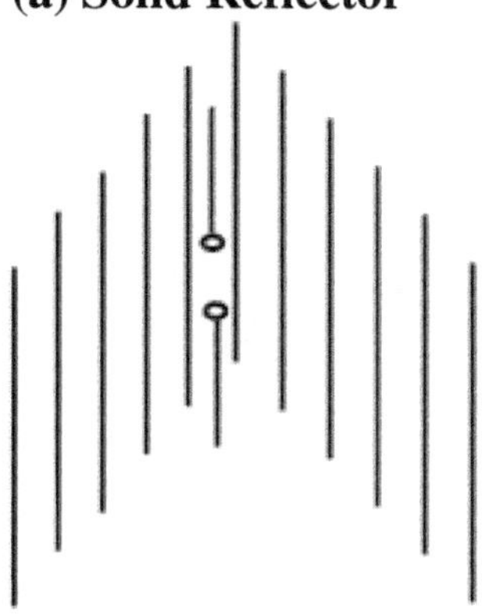

(b) Wire Reflector

Figure 1.3 Corner – Reflector Antennas

The characteristic feature of corner antenna includes moderately high gain. The pattern feature of it is that the forward (main beam) gain is much higher that the gain in the opposite direction. This is termed as front-to back ratio, which is evident from it radiation pattern portrayed in Figure 1.4

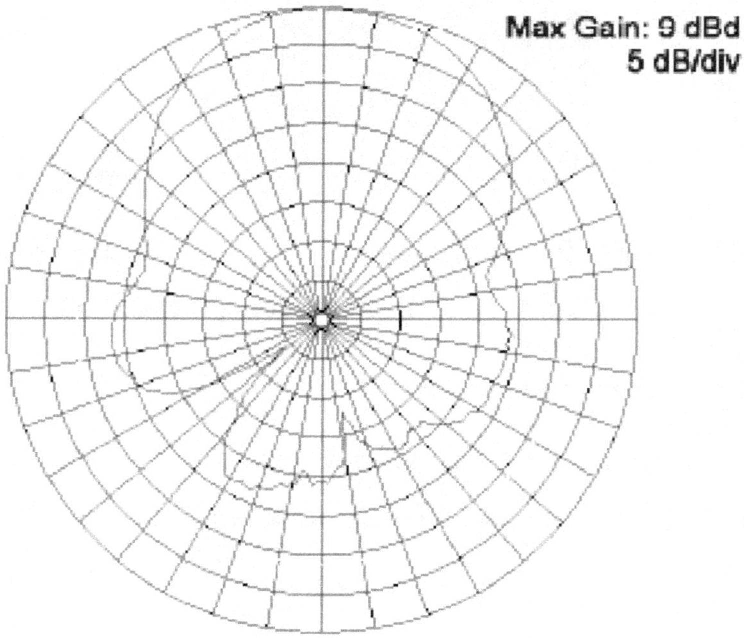

Figure 1.4 Radiation Pattern in Horizontal Plane of Corner – Reflector

1.3.1.3 Yagi Antenna

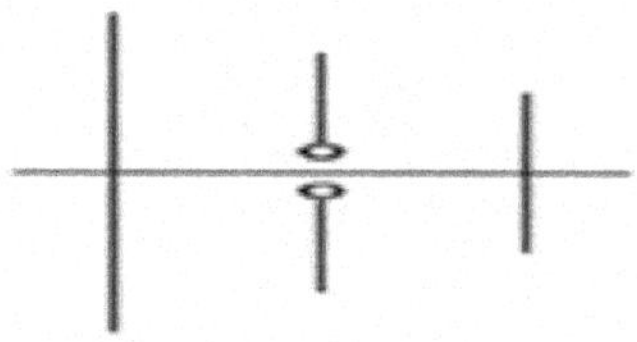

(a) 3 Element

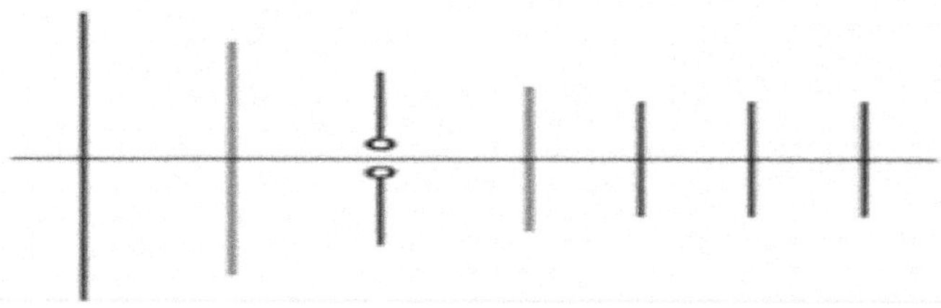

(b) Multi Element

Figure 1.5 Yagi Antenna Structures

Yagi antenna is a type of antenna design that uses passive elements. Figure 1.5 illustrates the structure of Yagi antenna. It can be constructed with one or more reflector elements and director elements. Figure 1.5 (a) and 1.5 (b) shows a Yagi antenna with one reflector, a folded-dipole active element and seven directors, mounted for horizontal polarization. Figure 1.6 illustrates a typical Yagi antenna.

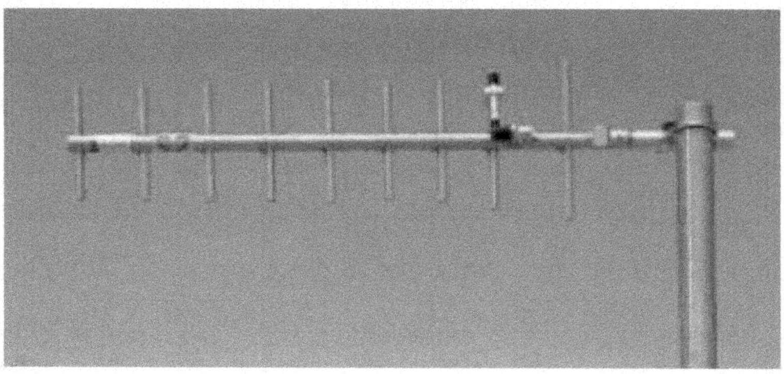

Figure 1.6 A typical Yagi antenna

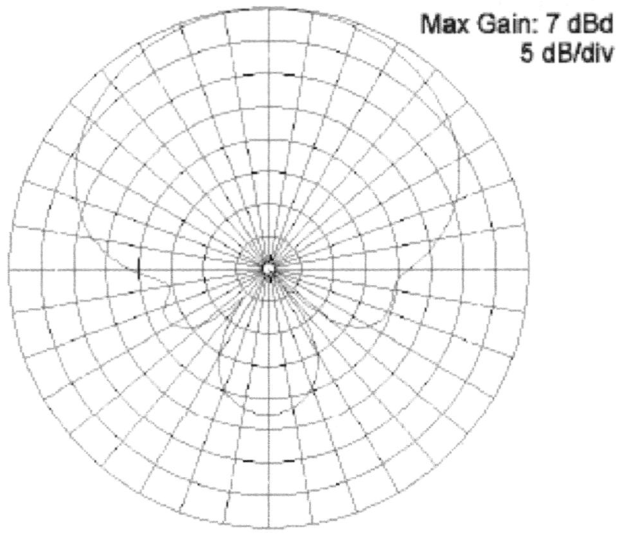

Figure 1.7 Horizontal Radiation Pattern of Yagi Antenna

The radiation pattern of the Yagi antenna in horizontal plane is shown in Figure 1.7. The pattern shown is obtained for a three element i.e. one reflector, one active element and one director elements Yagi antenna. In general, the gain of the Yagi antenna increases and bandwidth becomes narrower with increase in the number of elements. It can be mounted to support either vertical or horizontal polarization. It is used normally for point-to-point applications, as between a base station and repeater station sites.

1.3.2 Classification Based on Characteristics and Applications

1.3.2.1 Wire Antennas

Wire antennas are the fundamentally used and seen everywhere on automobiles, buildings, ships, and aircraft and so on. Dipole, loop and helix are the various shapes of wire antenna. The basic wire antenna is the short dipole antenna which is a short wire. Loop antennas can be of any form including circular, rectangle, square, ellipse, or any other configuration. Due to simplicity, circular loop configuration is mostly preferred.

1.3.2.2 Aperture Antennas

Aperture antennas are preferred to match the increasing demand for sophistication and to cover higher frequency ranges. These antennas are widely used in aircraft and spacecraft applications, as they can be conveniently mounted on the skin of the aircraft or spacecraft. By providing proper shielding with a dielectric material, these antennas can be protected from hazardous conditions of the environment.

1.3.2.3 Array Antennas

Radiation characteristics play a vital role in the antenna's selection. It may not be achieved by a single element. The cumulative electrical and geometrical arrangement of radiating elements will result in desirable radiation characteristics. The arrangement of arrays causes radiation to be maximum in one direction and minimum in others or otherwise as desired. Such antennas which posses an assembly of radiators mounted on a continuous structure to form an array are termed as array antennas.

1.3.2.4 Reflector Antennas

In long distance communication systems, sophisticated forms are to be used in order to transmit and receive signals. These signals travel up to a distance of millions of miles. The antennas designed with large diameters find to be suitable for these applications. The diameters are as large as 305m. Increase in dimension results in improved gain to receive or transmit the signals. These antennas are reflector antennas.

1.3.2.5 Lens Antennas

The diversion of energy in undesired directions can be prevented using lenses. The appropriate shaping of the geometrical configuration and selection of materials for the lenses makes them to transform various forms of divergent energy into plane waves. The antennas made with such lenses are termed as lens antennas. They are extensively used as parabolic reflectors, especially at high frequencies. At low frequencies, their dimensions and weight remarkably increase. These lens antennas are classified based on the material from which they are constructed or according to their geometrical shape.

1.3.2.6 Microstrip Antennas

Microstrip antennas or Microstrip Patch Antennas are used in high-performance applications viz. aircraft, spacecraft, satellite, missile applications etc. These antennas are preferred in applications where there are too many constraints like weight, cost, performance, installation, aerodynamic profile, low profile etc. These constraints form the fundamental requirement for mobile radio and wireless communication systems. To meet these specifications, microstrip antennas are used.

Microstrip antennas are planar resonant cavities that leak from their edges and radiate. The conducting patch separated by a dielectric substrateon a ground plane, forms the microstrip antenna. Printed circuit techniques can be used to etch the antennas on soft substrates to produce low-cost and repeatable antennas in a low profile. The antennas fabricated on compliant substrates withstand tremendous shock and vibration environments. Manufacturers for mobile communication base stations often fabricate these antennas directly in sheet metal and mount them on dielectric posts or foam in a variety of ways to eliminate the cost of substrates and etching. This also eliminates the problem of radiation from surface waves excited in a thick dielectric substrate used to increase bandwidth. A microstrip antenna is characterized by its Length, Width, Input impedance, and Gain and radiation patterns. Various parameters of the microstrip antenna and its design considerations were discussed in the subsequent sections of this Thesis.

1.4 MICRSOSTRIP PATCH ANTENNA

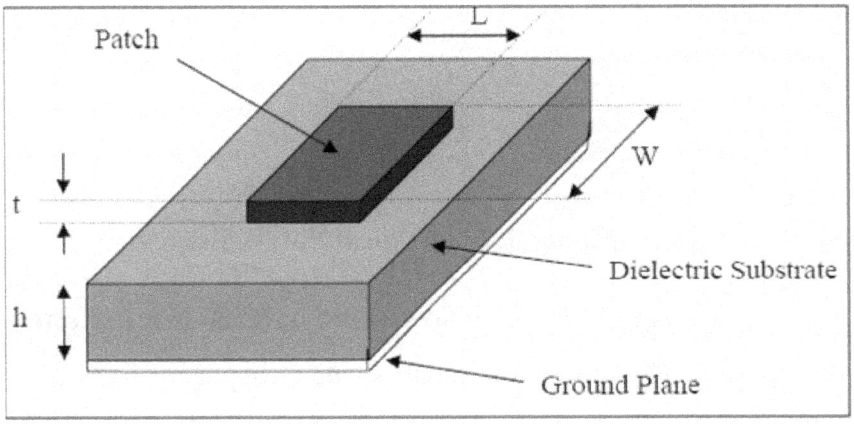

Figure 1.8 Microstrip Patch Antennas

The basic form of a Microstrip patch antenna has been displayed in Figure1.8. The figure 1.8 depicts that the structure of microstrip antenna has a radiating patch made available dielectric substrate and ground plane on the each side. Copper or gold of any form of shape can be used as a conducting material for the patch. This antenna has radiating and input lines(feed) fixed in the dielectric substrate. Arrays of antennas can be photo etched on the substrate, along with their feeding networks. Microstrip circuits make a wide variety of antennas possible through the use of the simple photo etching techniques. A normal transmission line radiates little power because the fringing fields are matched by nearby counteracting fields. Power radiates from open circuits and from discontinuities such as corners, but the amount depends on the radiation conductance load to the line relative to the patches.

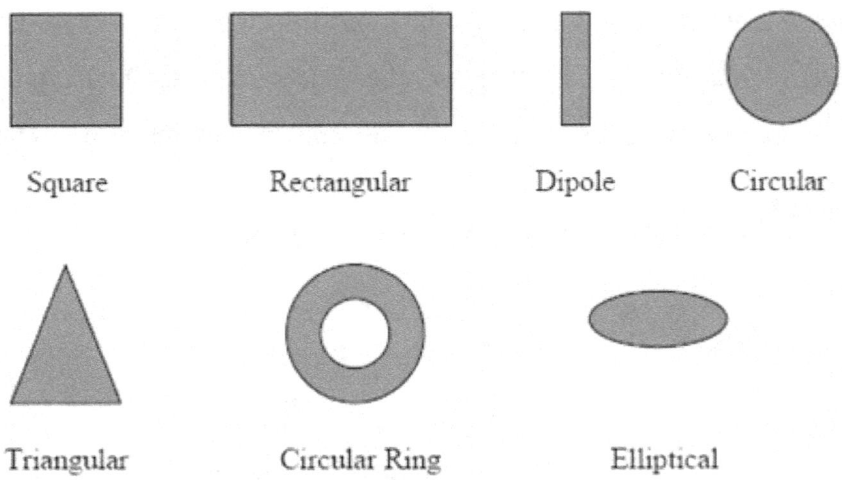

Figure 1.9 Typical Patch Shapes

To simplify the analysis and predict the performance of the microstrip antennas, any of the patch shapers displayed in Figure 1.9 can be used. The length 'L' of the rectangular patch is usually 0.3333 $\lambda_0 < L < 0.5\ \lambda_0$, where $\lambda_0$is the free-space wavelength. The patch is selected to be very thin such that $t << \lambda_0$, where 't' is the patch thickness. The height 'h' of the dielectric substrate is usually $0.003\ \lambda_0 \leq h \leq 0.05\ \lambda_0$. The dielectric constant of the substrate (ε_r) is typically in the range $2.2 \leq \varepsilon_r \leq 12$.

1.4.1 Applications of Microstrip Patch Antennas

The low-profile structure of microstrip patch antennas make them to be popular and compatible to be used in various handheld wireless devices such as cellular phones, pagers etc. in bio-medical instrumentation, telemetry and missile communication systems, and antenna should be thin and conformal. This make the microstrip patch antenna ease of use in satellite communication systems.

1.4.2 Merits and Drawbacks of Patch Antennas

The major advantages of microstrip patch antennas have been listed as follows:

- Low profile planar configuration
- Low fabrication cost.
- Supports Linear and circular polarization.
- Light weight.
- Low volume.
- Ease of integration with microwave integrated circuits (MICs).
- Accomplish dual and triple frequency operations.
- Vigorous when equestrian on rigid surfaces.

The major drawbacks of microstrip antennas are:

- Bandwidth is very narrow.
- Poor efficiency
- Very low Gain
- Unnecessary radiation from feeds and junctions
- Tapered slot antennas may exhibit poor end fire radiator
- Very small power handling capability
- Excitation from the wave surface.

1.5 FEED TECHNIQUES

In microstrip patch antennas, the feed technique decides the power transfer between the strip and the radiating patch. The feed techniques of microstrip antennas can be classified into two categories as contact and non-contact methods. In the contact method, the power at Radio Frequency (RF) is fed straight to the radiating patch, through a connecting component viz. a microstrip line. In the non – contact method, the transfer of power between the microstrip line and the patch happens through the coupling formed due to electromagnetic field.

In particular, contact methods of feed techniques arewidely used in the microstrip line and coaxial probe, whereas the aperture coupling and proximity coupling types belong to the non-contact method of feed technique.

1.5.1 Microstrip Line Feed

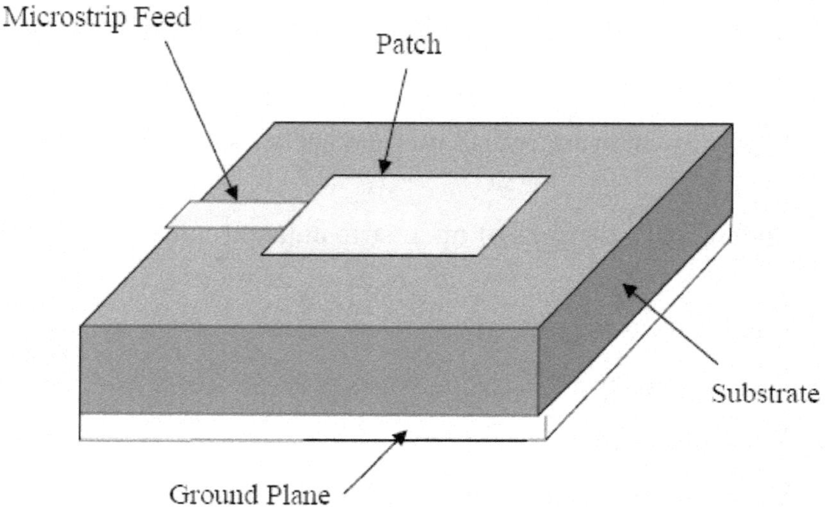

Figure 1.10 Microstrip Line Feed

The microstrip line feed technique, is a contact type feed technique and is portrayed in Figure 1.10. It consists of a conducting strip linked straight to the verge of the microstrip patch. The width of the conducting strip is less compared to the patch. The importance of low width is that the planar structure can be obtained by etching the feed on the same substrate. The patch and its corresponding inset cut match the impedance of the feed line. This technique removes the need for additional impedance matching element. The control of impedance is effected through the inset position. This makes the microstrip line feed technique offers comfort of fabrication and ease in modelling and impedance matching. The feed radiation of this type leads to undesired cross polarized radiation, which is the major drawback of the microstrip line feed. Increasing the thickness of the dielectric substrate results in increased surface waves and false feed radiation, this fetters the bandwidth of the antenna.

1.5.2 Coaxial Feed

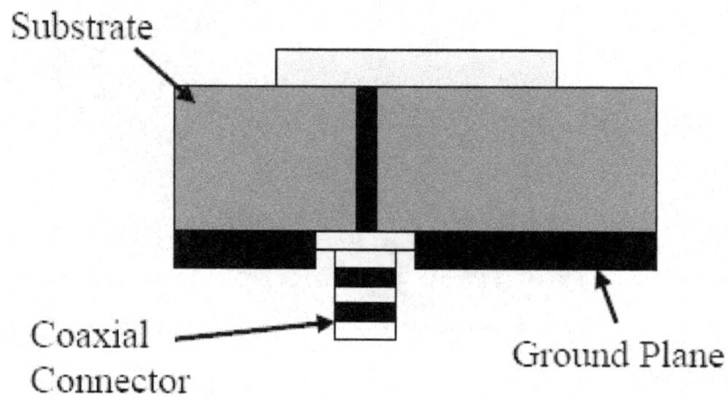

Figure 1.11 Coaxial Feed

The most commonly used feed technique is the coaxial feed or probe feed portrayed in Figure 1.11. As depicted in the figure, the connector of the coaxial of the connector is supply the input over the dielectric substrate then is soldered to the patch radiation. Ground plane and outer connecter are joined together with the radiation patch. In addition, this method has ease of fabrication and evolves low false radiation.

Narrow bandwidth, drilling a hole in the substrate making it difficult to model and the protruding connector outside the ground plane, makes it to be completely planar for thick substrates ($h > 0.02\lambda_0$) can be recorded as the drawbacks of the coaxial feed technique. In case of thicker substrate, the increase length causes the input impedance to be more inductive. This leads to matching problems. In general, it is observed that for thick dielectric substrates both the microstrip line feed and coaxial feed suffer from numerous shortcomings.

1.5.3 Aperture Coupled Feed

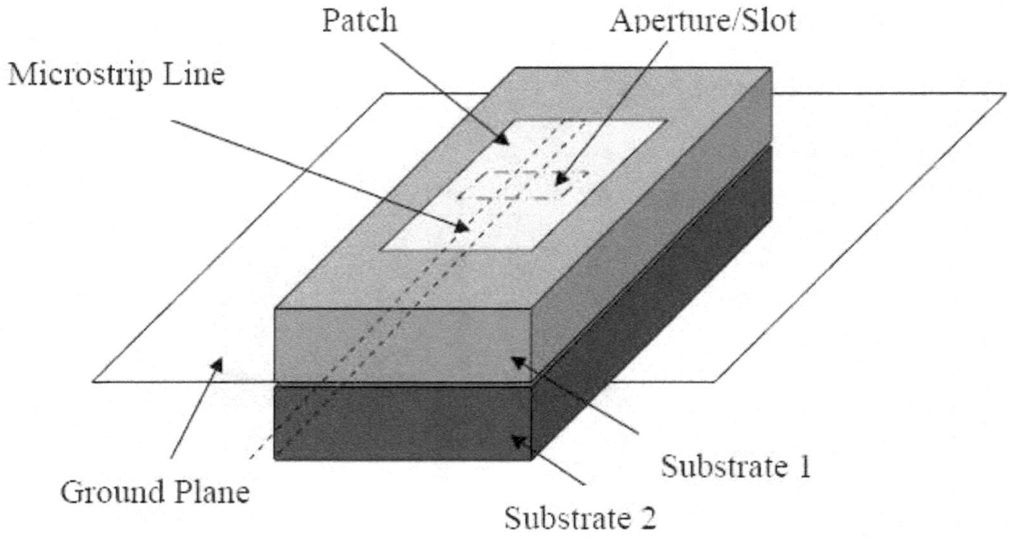

Figure 1.12 Aperture Coupled Feed

In aperture coupled feed, the radiating patch and the microstrip feed line are separated by the ground plane as shown in Figure 1.12. The aperture in the ground plane or a slot provides the coupling between the patch and the feed line. The symmetrical configuration provides lower cross polarization as because the coupling aperture is centred under the patch. The shape, size and location of the aperture determine the amount of coupling from the feed line to the patch. The spurious radiation is minimized, since the ground plane separates the patch and the feed line. In order to optimize radiation for the patch, a high dielectric material is used for bottom dielectric and a thick low dielectric constant material is used for the top substrate. The aperture couple feed technique has multiple layers to be fabricated and provides narrow bandwidth. These are is the major drawbacks of this feed scheme.

1.5.4 Proximity Coupled Feed

Proximity coupled feed technique is also termed as electromagnetic coupling scheme. The construction of this feed scheme is shown in Figure 1.13. It is made of tow dielectric substrates. The feed line lies between tow substrates and the radiating patch is on the top of the upper substrate. The thickness of the microstrip antenna increases when the proximity coupled feed technique is used. This increase in thickness eliminates spurious feed radiation and provides very high bandwidth. The range of bandwidth is approximately 13%. These are the advantages of this feed technique.

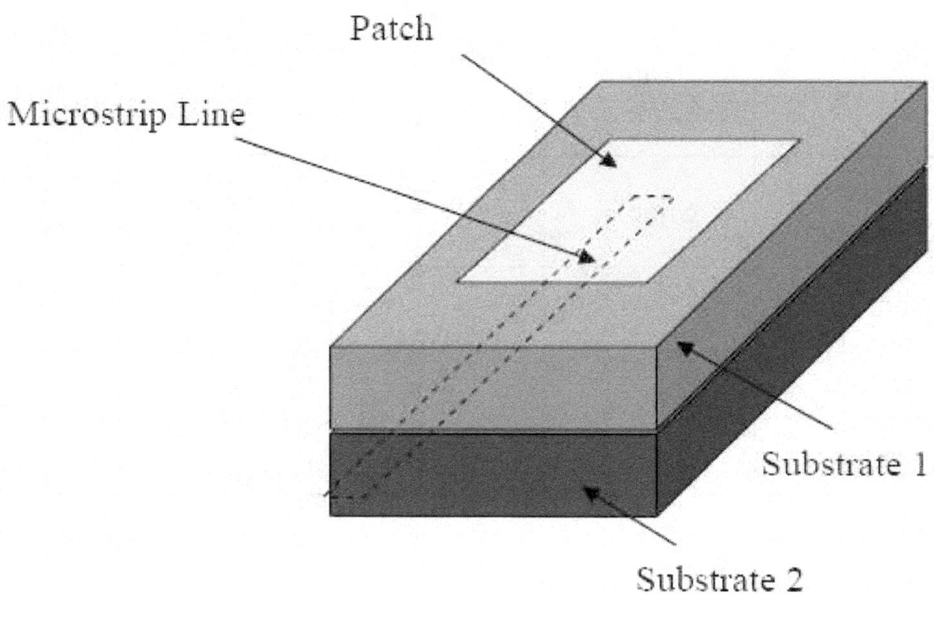

Figure 1.13 Proximity Coupled Feed

In order to match the impedance, the length and width to line ratio of the feed line has to be controlled. This makes the two dielectrics to be aligned properly, and so the fabrication becomes difficult. This in turn increases the thickness of the antenna. These are the shortcomings of the proximity couple feed technique. The comparison of the various different feed schemes have been tabulated in Table 1.1

Table 1.1 Comparison of Different Feed Methods

Parameters or Properties	Microstrip Line Feed	Coaxial Feed	Aperture Coupled Feed	Proximity Coupled Feed
Unauthentic radiation level	High	High	Low	Very low
Reliability	Better Reliability	Soldering results in poor reliability	Best reliability	Good
Complexity of Fabrication	Simple	Needs soldering and drilling	Requires alignment	Requires alignment
Impedance Matching	Simple	Simple	Simple	Simple
Bandwidth achieved through impedance matching	2.01% to 5.05%	2.01% to 5.05%	2.01% to 5.05%	14%

1.6 PERFORMANCE PARAMETERS OF ANTENNAS

To evaluate the performance of an antenna, the properties such as radiation pattern, directivity, gain, bandwidth, polarization and radiation intensity are to be studied.

1.6.1 Radiation Pattern

The mathematical or graphical representation of the radiation properties of the antenna when defined as a function of space coordinates is termed as antenna radiation pattern. It is also called as antenna pattern, which is determined in the far field region and represented by the directional coordinate functions. The radiation properties include power flux density, radiation intensity, field strength, directivity, phase or polarization.

1.6.2 Radiation Intensity

Radiation intensity, is defined as, “the power radiated from an antenna per unit solid angle”. It is the product of radiation intensity and the square of the distance, expressed in Equation 1.1.

$$U = r^2 w_{rad} \qquad (1.1)$$

Where,

U = Radiation Intensity, watt per steradian

r = distance in m

ω_{rad} = Solid angle in radians

1.6.3 Directivity

The ratio of radiation intensity in a particular direction from the antenna to the averaged intensity in all directions is termed as directivity of an antenna. The Directivity of antenna is derived as from Equation 1.2,

$$D = \frac{U}{U_O} \tag{1.2}$$

Where,

D – Directivity

U – Radiation intensity watt per steradian

U_O- Radiation intensity in every direction

P_{rad} – Radiated power in W

1.6.4 Gain of Antennas

The ratio of the intensity to the radiation intensity in a given direction, is called as Antenna Gain. It is obtained only if the antenna's accepted power is radiated isotropically. The gain of an antenna is determined as per the Equation 1.3.

$$Gain = 4\pi \frac{Raddiation\ indensity}{Total\ input\ power} \tag{1.3}$$

1.6.5 Bandwidth of Antennas

The range of frequencies on which the antenna's performance are relevant to some characteristics and conforms to a specific standard, is called as bandwidth of the antenna. The characteristics viz. input impedance, polarization, radiation efficiency, pattern and gain of the antenna are to be considered over the bandwitdth on the either side of the center frequency. The value of these performance parameters should be within permissible value at the center frequency. Bandwidth is calculated by per Equation 1.4 as,

$$Bandwidth = \frac{f_H - f_L}{f_C} \times 100\% \tag{1.4}$$

Where,

f_H = Higher Cut-off frequency in Hz

f_L = Lower Cut-off frequency in Hz

f_c = Center frequency in Hz

1.6.6 Polarization

The divergence of the wave transmitted or radiated by an antenna in a given direction is defined as Polarization of an antenna. The polarization can be assumed to be in the direction of maximum gain, when the direction is not mentioned. The phenomenon by which the electromagnetic wave in time-varying direction and the relative magnitude of the vector are mentioned as a function of time at a fixed location and traced and observed along the propagation direction is called as polarization of a radiated wave. The types of polarization of antenna are,

(1) Linear or Plane Polarization

(2) Circular Polarization

(3) Elliptical Polarization

1.7 ANTENNA DESIGN PROCEDURE:

The design of antenna includes the determination of length and width of the patch. The design procedure assumes that the specified information includes dielectric constant of the substrate (ε_r), the resonant frequency of antenna (f_r), and the height of the substrate (h). The procedure is as follows:

Specify

- Dielectric constant of the substrate (ε_r)
- Resonant frequency of the antenna (f_r)
- Height of the substrate (h)

Determine

- Width of the patch (W)
- Length of the patch (L)

1.8 PROBLEM IDENTIFICATION AND OBJECTIVE

The design of the antennas making them suitable for wireless communication applications, discussed in the previous section, reveals that an optimal antenna design is the need of the hour. The design should be such that the antenna upshots the drawbacks of the existing antennas in terms of performance indices viz. Gain, voltage standing wave ratio (VSWR) and pass bandwidths.

1.9 MOTIVATION

The various research studies cited here points that how a compact microstrip line-fed ultra-wide band antennas incorporating triple notched band has to be investigated, thereby fabricated. The antenna has to be operated in different modes to incorporate the frequency bands of Wi-Max, WLAN and X-band Satellite Communications. From the literature studies, it is inferred that in recent years, the need for multiband antenna grows radically. In addition, there arises a necessity to suggest a compact single layer microstrip line fed double U-slot patch antenna. This is to achieve multiple bands and wide bandwidth. The antenna designed has to be compact and should have unique structure.

1.10 OBJECTIVES OF THE RESEARCH WORK

The main objective of the proposed research work is to design, analyze, develop, fabricate and test the performance of antennas that suits wireless communication systems. The research work is to improve the scalability and availability of the proposed 3 antenna schemes of interest. The research has been focused and carried out to significantly improve the efficiency of the antenna schemes based on return loss, pass bandwidth and gain. By this way, the radiation pattern and polarization are enhanced

The research objectives are as follows:

- Extensively review the available antenna designs
- To design and evaluate a compact microstrip line-fed ultra-wide band antenna encompassing triple notched band.
- To design and analyse a compact single-layer microstrip line fed multifunctional patch antenna with U-slots to get multiple bands and wide bandwidth.
- To Propose a compact CPW-fed triple-band antenna for GSM, Wi-Fi and Wi-Max applications
- The proposed antenna systems are to be fabricated and tested.
- Analyze the performance of the proposed antenna designs.
- Demonstrate the superiority of the characteristics exhibited by the proposed antenna schemes for wireless communication applications.

1.11 ORGANIZATION OF THE THESIS

The association of the thesis is the design of an effective antenna for wireless communication system. This thesis is organized into seven chapters.

The introductory to the fundamental definition of antenna, types and feed techniques, parameters for performance evaluation, design parameters, related works, and problem identification were dealt in **Chapter 1**. The motivation behind the development of the proposed designs and the objectives of the research work has also been discussed. **Chapter 2** describes the literature survey of design and performance analysis of the antenna types taken up for study. The design, analysis and performance assessment of compact microstrip line-fed ultra-wide band antenna encompassing triple notched band has been dealt in **Chapter 3.**

Chapter 4 elaborates the design and analysis of triple band notched antenna with double U-Slots. In **Chapter 5**the design, analysis and performance evaluation of the compact single-layer micro-strip line fed multifunctional patch antenna with U-slots have been discussed.The proposed compact CPW-fed triple band antenna design aspects, analysis and performance estimation has been detailed in **Chapter 6.**

Chapter 7evaluates the performance aspects of all the antenna designs taken up for study. The superiority of the proposed compact single-layer microstrip line fed multifunctional patch antenna with U-slots for effective wireless communication system has been demonstrated. **Chapter 8** summarizes the work presented in the thesis. The main contribution of the thesis is highlighted and suggestions are made for future work.

CHAPTER 2

LITERATURE STUDIES

2.1 INTRODCUTION

This chapter depicts the extensive survey of the literature available on the various antenna configurations intended to be studied in this research work. The issues addressed by various researchers, the methodology to solve them which includes, the design, simulation model and the analysis of the results have been presented to a greater extent. The antenna scheme that have been included in the literature studies are compact single layer with single U-slot, triple band single layer double U-slot antenna, multifunctional mutlipatch microstrip antenna and compact CPW-fed microstrip antenna systems. The various types of antennas, their feed techniques, and design and evaluation parameters have been addressed in Chapter 1.

2.2 BACKGROUND STUDIES OF COMPACT MICROSTRIP LINE FEED ULTRA-WIDE BAND ANTENNA

A compact planar ultra-wide Band (ULTRA-WIDE BAND) antenna has been researched by Qing – Xin Chinu and Ying-Ying Yang (2008). In their work, they studied the antenna characteristics with (3.4Ghz to 5.5 GHz)both band are notched characteristics. This type of designed antenna included rectangular metal patch and also a 50 Ω coplanar waveguide (CPW) in the transmission line. This proposed antenna exhibited the band – rejected filtering properties, via the tow nested C-shaped slots in the patch. The design, simulation and measured parameters of the aimed configuration found most useful in WiMAX and WLAN applications, as they unveiled, the desired characteristics for these applications.

Antenna miniaturization is becoming quite popular among the researchers. It reduces the size and enhances the performance parameters. The studies carried by Damir Zayniyev and Djuradj Budimir (2010) revealed the same. They integrated multiband antennas with dual-band filter. This integration suppressed the unwanted harmonics of antenna and improved the reflection loss and selectivity of the antenna. Nowadays communication systems use two or more frequency bands. For instance, WLAN standard IEEE 802.11 operates at 2.4 to 2.45 gigahertz and 5.15 to 5.85 gigahertz. The WiMAX IEEE 802.16 operates at 2.3 to 2.7 gigahertz, 3.3 to 3.9 gigahertz and 5.15 to 5.85 gigahertz. The integrated antenna systems have been identified as the best solution for these sorts of applications.

A compact dual band filter antenna subsystem addressed by Umair Naeem *et al.* (2010), resulted by implementing stepped impedance resonator filter to a hybrid dual band antenna. The filter is incorporated using Low Temperature Co-fired Ceramics technology (LTCC), on a half cylindrical planar monopole antenna to achieve the dual band response. The anticipated results have been achieved by the researchers. The increased band of operation made the antenna systems to be used widely in many wireless communication systems. Cheung S *et al.* (2010) utilized a three pairs of meandered ground stubs and created triple band-notched characteristics. This has been addressed for a compact planar monopole antenna used in the ultra-wide band. The three bands of operation achieved includes IEEE 802.16 (WiMAX) band (3.3-3.6 GHz), the lower wireless area network (WLAN) band (5.15-5.35 GHz) and the higher WLAN band (5.725-5.825 GHz). In this research work, it is evident that the center frequencies and bandwidths of the notches can be adjusted by adjusting the dimensions of the meandered ground stubs. The research work has been supported by a designed, fabricated and tested prototype model.

Wei-Jun Wu *et al.* (2011) designed, fabricated, measured the parameters and validated the results of a new compact filter-antenna for modern wireless communication systems. The designed antenna system consisted of two microstrip square open-loop resonators, a coupled line and a Γ-shaped antenna. These three components are integrated be a filter antenna. When the Γ-shaped antenna is excited by a coupled line it becomes as the admittance inverter in filter design and performs as a radiator and last resonator of the bandpass filter. The proposed design of this research studies, followed the circuit approach synthesis and the measured performance indices implied that this type of filter antenna achieved an impedance bandwidth of 16.3% (over 2.26-2.66 GHz) at a reflection coefficient | S 11 | <; - 10 dB and has a gain of 2.41 dBi.

Yahng Lu *et al.* (2011) reduced the ground-plane effects on ultra-wide band monopole antennas, which were found to be a common problem with ultra-wide band monopole antenna. The identified problem has been resolved by introducing slots along the top edge of the ground. The authors developed an equivalent circuit model, and studied the behavior of the slots. Validation of the proposed methodology has been done by comparing the simulated and experimental hardware results. Chao-Tang Chuang and Shyh-Jong Chung (2011) synthesized and designed new printed filtering antenna. This antenna structure has been presented to meet the requirement of efficient integration and simple fabrication. The researchers introduced a new Co-Design approach of integration has been utilized to integrate the filter and antenna. In the prototype model, a printed inverted-L antenna and the parallel coupled microstrip line sections have been used to illustrate the synthesis of a bandpass filtering antenna. The inverted-L antenna suggested by them consists of series RLC circuits, which performed as a radiator and last resonator of the bandpass filter. The investigators proposed the step by step procedure for the implementation of the filter design specifications. The proposed structure evidenced that the accuracy and filter capacity of the designed antenna has been improved to a greater extent. The performance indices taken up for study to validate the design of this prototype include return loss, total radiated power and the plot between radiation gains versus frequency.

The C and U shaped slots of the dual frequency ultra wide band antenna have been addressed by Ojaroudi and Ebarhimian (2012). The authors studied that the insertion of these two pair of U-shaped slots in the ground plane and addition of arc-shaped (C – shaped) parasitic strips around the radiating element, achieved two notched frequency bands in the WiMAX and WLAN frequency bands. The voltage standing wave ratio (VSWR) of <2 has been recorded in their experimental results. The two highly rejected band frequencies of the proposed antenna have been observed in the frequency region of 3.3–3.7GHz and 5–6GHz. Similar work has been carried out by Cheng Wang *et al.* (2012), with C-shaped and U-shaped slots. In this model, the researchers identified that by adjusting the length and location of the slots, the notched frequency bands can be adjusted. Their design also exhibited better performance characteristics with good radiation pattern and gains in the operating bands.

Yun-Jui Lee *et al.* (2012) designed a compact dual-band filtering microstrip antenna with the same polarization planes for WLAN bands. The planed design comprised of a slot-loaded patch and a half-wavelength stepped impedance resonator with the same aperture ground. The proposed system has been simulated using HFSS and the coupling coefficient has been extracted to determine the physical dimension of the apertures. The antenna designed provided good selectivity and same polarization planes in the frequency bands of 2.4 GHz and 5.2 GHz. A dual band-notched

A novel planar ultra-wide band antenna addressed by Wen Jiang and Wenquan Che (2012), with dual notched bands found more suitable for WIMAX and Wi-Fi applications. This proposed antenna configuration consisted of a square patch and a modified grounded plane. In this design, a T-shaped stub has been embedded in the square slot of the radiation patch and a pair of U-shaped parasitic strips has been used beside the feed line. These changes in the design resulted in dual notched bands characteristics. The significance of this antenna scheme is that it offered high rejection level in the stop band. The scheme also provided wide bandwidth of 2.8 GHz to 11.0 GHz, with two notched bands of 3.3-4.0 GHz for WiMAX and 5.05–5.90 GHz for WLAN applications.

The literature studies mentioned so far implies that filtering plays a vital role in deciding the notch-band of an antenna. The research work of Araghi Amin and Waladi Vorya (2013) evidenced the same. They proposed a Defected Ground Structure (DGS) and a radiating patch with arc shaped step. This design is notched by removing two squares at the bottom. They also modified the DGs structure as shovel-shaped and achieved band-notched characteristics that involved operating frequency band of Dedicated Short-Range Communication (DSRC) systems and WLAN. The key features of the proposed antenna scheme are omnidirectional H-pane radiation pattern and appropriate impedance characteristics. The results exhibited are recorded as VSWR < 2 with notch frequency band at 5.13 to 6.1 GHz.

Coplanar Waveguide (CPW) fed dual band-notched antennas become popular owing to their superior characteristics in wireless communication applications. Xiang long Liu *et al.* (2013) proposed a CPW-fed dual band notched WUB antenna. This antenna configuration comprised of a pair of bended dual – L shaped parasitic branches, with circular slotted ground. The advantage of dual – L bended shape structures is that they offer tow notched bands when attached in the slotted ground. The authors explained that parameter of antenna augmenting the lengths and positions of the designed branches, the desired operating of the notch-bands of WLAN and WiMAX can be obtained in the antenna. The experimental result validated the simulation results of this proposed antenna arrangement.

The authors Xiang long Liu *et al.* (2013 a) in their next study presented a novel printed microstrip-fed monopole ultra-wideband antenna with dual notch-band. In this work, they inserted a meandering sot between the feed-line and radiation patch. By this they generated a lower notch-band of 3.3 GHz to 3.7 GHz. Additionally, they embedded a pair of symmetrical C-shaped strips. This design generated an upper notch-band of 5.15 GHz to 5.85 GHz. In the investigation studies of Rezaul Azim *et al.* (2013) a dual band-notch characteristics have been resulted from a planar slot antenna. The arrangement of this proposed antenna comprised of a rectangular tuning stub and a ground plane with tapered-shape slot. An angle-shaped parasitic slit is etched in the rectangular tuning stub to create a notched band for WiMAX. To achieve the bands for WLAN applications, two symmetrical parasitic slits have been placed inside the slot of the ground plane. The notched bands of the proposed scheme helped to mitigate the possible interference between ultra-wide band and the narrow bands.

Planar ultra-wide band monopole antenna with dual band-notched characteristics can be designed by inserting a pair of two slots in the ground plane and appending it with a pair of arc-shaped parasitic strips around the radiating element. This structure resulted with two notched-band frequencies for WiMAX and WLAND applications. These have been the findings of the examination carried out by Mohamad Yazdi and Nader Komjani (2013). Ahmed T M *et al.* (2013) presented the design of a dual frequency-notch ultra-wide banddesigned antenna by means of the easy and simple parasitic slits. The notch band in this type of configuration is obtained by etching one angle-shaped parasitic slit on the tuning stub for WiMAX and appending tow symmetrical parasitic slits on the slot of the ground plane. The design and experimental results of this research work have been found to be in line with the studies made by Rezaul Azim *et al.* (2013). Junhui-H Wang *et al.* (2013) also suggested a similar design work.

Samavia Haroon *et al.* (2014) proposed a low profile ultra-wide band antenna with triple band characteristics. This proposed design is a coplanar waveguide fed radiator with incorporated notching resonators. The resonators have been etched to achieve the desired band rejection. The authors proposed three different notch antennas with single band rejection for each antenna. The design has been approached by a new technique termed Sequential Design ofultra-wide band antenna. By this approach, an optimized design is achieved by accumulating the three stop band resonators in a single design. The proposed design has been capable of operating at the frequency range of 2.4 GHZ to 11 GHZ. The simulated and measured results fulfilled the performance criteria for the wireless applications.

Rezaul Azim *et al.* (2014) designed a dual notched band ultra-wide bandantenna with single tri-arm resonator. A single tri-arm resonator has been etched in order to achieve band – notch characteristics. The experimental analyses of the authors implied that a wide bandwidth has been achieved of the range 2.98 GHz to 10.76 GHz. The return loss resulted has been observed as $\leq$ 10 dB. The notched bands operate at 3.5 GHz and 5.5 GHz. In order to control the dual notched bands, the proposed scheme has been implemented with a simple filter element, which resulted in better performance characteristics for ultra-wide band applications. Ruina Lian *et al.* (2015) proposed and investigated on a low profile dual polarized stepped slot antenna array for base station. The antenna configuration suggested by them composed of two pairs of stepped-impedance slots, that are being excited by two orthogonal stepped microstrip feed lines. In this system, the combination of fundamental and spurious resonances of the stepped-impedance slot resonators, offered broadband characteristics. The introduction of shorting pins in the design provided good cross polarization. These two design modifications resulted in a four-element antenna array, which has been simulated and experimentally tested. The results demonstrated that this scheme of interest offered bandwidth of 46% in the range 1.55 to 2.5 GHz and 39.7% in the frequency range of 1.69 GHz to 2.5 GHz, respectively for Port 1 and Port 2. The cross-polarization level of the scheme has been maintained at a level lower than -27 dB. The horizontal and vertical polarization gains have been measured as 13.5 dBi and 13.9 dBi respectively.

Le Kang *et al.* (2015) illustrated the working of a compact multiple-input-multiple-output antenna. This antenna configuration composes of two offset microstrip fed antenna elements and is placed perpendicular to each other to achieve high isolation and polarization diversity. The experimental results of this design offered an impedance bandwidth of 3.08 GHz to 11.8 GHz. The measured reflection coefficient is less than -10 dB, except the rejection band of 5.03 to 5.97 GHz. To validate the suitability of proposed MIMO antenna scheme forultra-wide band applications, the port isolation, envelope correlation coefficient and radiation characteristics have been investigated. A switchable 3-D-Coverage-phase array antenna package for 5th Generation (5G) mobile terminals have been investigated by Naser Ojaroudiparchin *et al.* (2016). In this investigated antenna scheme, three identical subarrays of patch antennas have been arrange compactly such that a broad three-dimensional scanning coverage is achieved. The proposed design resulted with a high gain of > -10 dB gain, with goo directivity and efficiency. These results reflected that this proposed antenna system can be efficiently used for 5G mobile communication systems.

A dual-polarized dual-mode orbital angular momentum (OAM) microstrip antenna array has been suggested by Hui Li *et al.* (2017). A four-element antenna array with specific excitation generated the OAM radio beam. This design scheme has been used to produce dual mode OAM waves. The measured results portrayed that the proposed antenna array achieved good impedance matching over the band of 5.4 to 5.6 GHz and a port-to-port isolation better than 25 dB. Dan Feng *et al.* (2017) investigated and analyzed a broadband low-profile circular-polarized antenna on an Artificial Magnetic Conductor (AMC), which acts as a reflector. This antenna scheme achieved circular polarization characteristics through 90° phase shift through a crossed dipole. The results show that the proposed circularly polarized antenna has wide bandwidth and AR bandwidth in the low profile condition. Eugean kim *et al.* (2018) too investigated on the low profile circular polarized antenna on the AMC reflector. Their design demonstrated that the proposed scheme achieved higher peak gain of more than 3.8 dB.

Studies of Hong-Wei Deng *et al.* (2018) on the broadband pattern reconfigurable filtering microstrip antenna with quasi-yagi structure revealed that this antenna system resulted in four resonant modes that can be adjusted independently. Of these four modes, three of them have been created by Multi-Mode Resonator (MMR) and one by the radiator. The results envisaged that the proposed scheme provides bandwidth of 25% at 5.2 GHz. Wenxing An *et al.* (2018) discussed the working of low-profile wideband slot-loaded patch antenna with multi-resonant modes. This antenna scheme offered impedance bandwidth of 52.7% for the frequency range of 1.62 GHz to 2.78 GHz. The average gain of the system has been measured as 6 dBi. Neng-Wu *et al.* (2018)

proposed the microstrip patch antenna with low profile and broad impedance bandwidth. The result of their studies inferred that the antenna has gained a broad impedance bandwidth of about 55% for the frequency range of 1.62 GHz to 285 GHz.

2.3 BACKGROUND STUDIES OF MULTIFUNCTIONAL PATCH ANTENNA SCHEMES

Multifunctional patch antennas play a vital role in communication systems to meet the system standards, owing to the reasons of simple structure, compactness and low manufacturing cost. These antenna configurations consist of U-slot, to achieve multi-band characteristics. Researchers paid attention to modify the design, by incorporating two or more U-slots. The effectiveness of the modified design is that, it provided good impedance matching and provided operating bands of several frequency ranges. Various approaches addressed below have been suggested by many researchers supplemented by their simulation and experimental results. These results ensured that the multifunctional patch antennas can be used effectively for wireless communication systems.

Huynh T and Lee K F (1995) discussed a single-layer single patch wideband microstrip antenna. This patch of the antenna has been designed in the form of a rectangle with a U-shaped slot. Their studies resulted that the proposed antenna scheme of them provided impedance bandwidth of the range 10% to 40%, without adding any parasitic patches. Fan Yang (2003) utilized Electromagnetic Band-Gap (EBG) structures to integrate microstrip antennas. These antenna schemes had mushroom like structure and this has been analyzed in the Finite Difference Time Domain (FDTD). The key feature of the EBG structure is that it suppresses the surface-wave by exhibiting the near field distribution of the electromagnetic waves. They found that the EBG structure inserted between the array elements reduced the mutual coupling. Cheung S W *et al.* (2010) studied the features of triple band –notched ultra-wide bandantenna using Meandered Ground Stubs (MGS). They measured the flat transfer function and constant group delay within the operating and excluding the notched bands. Their results inferred that the proposed antenna configuration can be made suitable for Ultra-wide band applications.

Lee K F *et al.* (2012) modified the structure of U-slot patch antenna in order to improve the performance of the antenna for ultra-wide bandapplications. They suggested this modified structure for wideband, dual and triple band operation with small and large frequency ratios and for circular polarization. Hassan Tariq Chattha *et al.* (2011) reduced the ground-plane effects of ultra-wide band monopole antenna. They designed a single – feed circularly polarized patch antenna at L-band incorporating the developed U-slot loaded patch technique. The fabricated antenna had a high dielectric constant substrate of ε_r which resulted in reasonable axial-ratio bandwidth. This system resulted in a gain of 4.5 dBi an axial-ratio bandwidth of 3.2%. A new compact filter-antenna for modern wireless communication systems have been proposed by Jiao-Jiao Xie *et al.* (2011). The planned antenna configuration has been designed, fabricated and the test results have been measured to demonstrate that the proposed scheme well suits for the aimed applications. The designed system integrated two microstrip square open loop resonators, a coupled line and a Γ-shaped antenna to forma a filter-antenna. This system when tested provided near-zero transition loss, with impedance bandwidth of 16.3% over the frequency range of 2.26 GHz to 2.66 GHz at a reflection coefficient | S 11 | <; - 10 dB and gain of 2.41 dBi.

Compact broadband crescent moon-shape patch pair antenna has been analyzed by Jingli Guo *et al.* (2011). This has been a novel compact wideband patch antenna and consisted of two simple patch airs with opposite phase feed. The result of the studies implied that the antenna has active reflection coefficient less than -9.6 dB in the band 2.6 GHz to 6 GHz. The radiation performance of the proposed antenna configuration aps0 found to be good over the whole frequency band. Lee K F *et al.* (2011) generalized the approach to design an antenna with U-slots for dual ad triple band patch antenna systems. They divided the U-slots embedded them in patches and in the matching band to create dual-band antenna. Along with it, another U-slot has been cut on the same patch to get triple – band antenna. They suggested this type of fabrication for L-probe and M-probe fed patch, coaxially fed and aperture-couple stacked patches. The results of both the proposed fabrication schemes have been in line with the original antenna design.

Multi-Input-Multi-Output (MIMO) antenna arrays pulled the interest of many researchers. Xue Ming Ling and Rong Lin Li (2011) devised a novel dual band MIMO antenna array. These antenna arrays had a low mutual coupling and were found to be useful for portable wireless devices. The MIMO antenna array had two back-to-back monopoles elements, a shorting strip and an isolation stub. These components reduced the mutual coupling and covered the WLAN bands of the frequency range 2.4 GHz to 5.8 GHz. The test results provided an isolation lower than 25 dB and 20 dB for 2.4 GHz and 5.8 GHz respectively. MU'ath J Al-Hasan *et al.* (2011) studied and presented a New Millimeter Wave (MMW), EBG structure for mutual coupling reduction. The EBG structure has been formed without the usage of metallic wires. It is formed by etching two slots and adding tow connecting bridges to a conventional uniplanar EBG unit-cell. The proposed EBG unit-cell provided 12% and more size reduction and also enhanced the performance and applicability to wireless communication systems.

Bo Li, *et al.* (2012) designed and investigated aultra-wide band printed antenna for the dual band-notched with C-shaped and a U-shaped slot for WLAN and WiMAX applications. This suggested antenna scheme consisted of a taper rectangular monopole antenna with new line feed for a frequency range of 2 GHz to 12 GHz. In this study, a comparative analysis has been made between the design approaches such as L shape slot, F shape feed line. The results benefitted that the novel feel line is suitable for multi-band and reconfigurable antenna. A designedultra-wide bandantenna with dual notched frequency bands for wireless communication (WiMAX and WLAN) applications has been investigated in the research work of Wen Jiang and Wenquan Che (2012). The novelty of this design is that it had a square patch and a modified grounded plane. In this design the dual notched band characteristics have been realized using a T-shaped stub embedded in the square slot of the radiation patch and a pair of U-shaped parasitic strips beside the line feed. The results of this antenna scheme made it suitable for WLAN and WiMAX applications. Sai Hoi Wong *et al.* (2013) suggested a single later single-patch dual band and triple band antennas, by cutting U-slots in the parch of a broad band antenna. The fabricated U-slot has been applied to L-Probe and M-Probe fed patches, coax-fed stacked patches and aperture coupled stacked patches. This design seemed to be complicated but resulted in both dual and triple band configurations. The main advantage is that the structures remain single-layer and single-patch. The feasibility of the design has been demonstrated by the simulation and experimental setups.

Radiation pattern of the antenna can be adjusted by adjusting the U-slots. The investigations made by Ahemed H Khidre and Kai-Fong Lee (2013) illustrated the same. They obtained two radiation beams by operating the patch antenna at the higher order mode instead of fundamental mode. It is achieved by using the U-slot technique. The simulation and experimental model analysis aided the performance of the systems. The studied antenna arrangement operated at a frequency range of 5.18 GHz to 5.95 GHz. The measured other performance indices include VSWR< 2, corresponding to

11.8% impedance bandwidth. The two radiation patterns exhibited were directed at 35° and -33° with 7.92 dBi and 5.94 dBi realized gain, respectively at 5.5 GHz. Ahmed Toaha Mobashsher *et al.* (2013) designed dual band notch ultra-wide band slot antenna by simple parasitic slits approach. This antenna structure is a planar slot antenna structure, whose components include rectangular tuning stub and a ground plane with tapered-shape slot. The notch bands have been created by etching one angle-shaped parasitic silt along the tuning stub and placing two symmetrical parasitic slits inside the slots of the ground plane. Adjustment of the size and location of the parasitic slits, achieved the ultra-wide bandoperating band without altering the antenna size. The benefit of this antenna scheme is that the notched bands aided to mitigate the inference between the ULTRA-WIDE BAND and narrow bands.

Bin Xu *et al.* (2013) devised a dual band-notched ultra-wide band antenna with circular slotted ground and fed with novel coplanar waveguide (CW). They attached a pair of bended dual L-shaped branches to the slot slotted ground. The trial and error optimization technique has been applied, to adjust the lengths and position of the branches. That resulted in the desired notch-bands for WLAN and WiMAX applications. A compact dual band-notched ultra-wide band antenna with meandering slot and C-shape strips has been addressed by Junhui H Wang *et al.* (2013). They inserted a meandering slot between the feed-line and radiation patch. This generated a lower notch-band at 3 GHz to 3.7 GHz. After addition of C-shaped strips to the feed-line, the higher notch band has been found to be generated of the range 5.15 GHz to 5.85 GHz. They concluded that the notch band can be adjusted by adjusting the position and placing of the two symmetrical strips. The experimental test results validated the design and simulated model.

Aykut Cihangir *et al.* (2014) proposed neutralized coupling elements for MIMO operations. This approach holds good for 4th Generation

(4G) mobile terminals. This system covered the low LTE700 and GSM 850/900 communication standards. The proposed configuration composed of two 3-D coupling elements, placed on a rectangular FR4 substrate. The neutralization technique has been applied to achieve high port-to-port isolation. The simulated and measured results of the fabricated system were found to be in good agreement with each other, making the system useful for 4G mobile applications. Amin Araghi and Vorya Waladi (2015), approached with a various and different method to analysis the design dual and triple frequency band antennas using U-slots on stacked patches. They studied the performance of the system using concerto software and observed that each U-slot will introduce a notch in corresponding matching band. They varied the feed positions and achieved the desired application within single antenna. They also rotated the planes of U-slots and studied the impact. The results portrayed that the antenna can be used for several applications in X band. Mallikarjuna *et al.* (2015) proposed an antenna design with combination of dual U-slot and multiple layers. This combination provided multiple bands and wide bandwidth. The thickness of the substrate on which the antenna has been fabricated is varied and the results have been observed. The proposed antenna provided triple bands of 1.6 GHz, 1.9 GHz and 3.8 GHz for a substrate thickness of 1.6 mm for a bandwidth of 600 MHz. The same configuration with 0.6 mm thickness resulted in 1.8 GHz, 2.2 GHz and 4.8 GHz for a bandwidth of 800 MHz. This proposed antenna scheme find wide useful for MMW wireless communication systems.

Bandwidth can be enhanced for a single-feed circularly polarized antenna using a metasurface. This has been illustrated by Nasimuddin *et al.* (2016). In their research work, a single-feed circularly polarized, rectangular slotted patch antenna has been suggested to enhance the bandwidth. This antenna scheme comprised of a rectangular slotted patch radiator and a metasurface with an array of rectangular - ring cells, and a coaxial feed. The metasurface helps to achieve wide circularly polarized bandwidth with a sevenfold size of a conventional antenna. The proposed antenna achieved VSWR < 2 and bandwidth of 36%. Patnam H Rao *et al.* (2017), designed and evaluated a multiband polarization shaped aperture antenna, which had various planar antennas embedded into a single footprint. The proposed arrangement had an L-probe fed suspended plate, horizontally polarized antenna, capable of operating at 900 MHz band. When the aperture is coupled and polarized vertically, the antenna operates at 4.2 GHz. This antenna system has been found to be suitable for airborne and Unmanned Aircraft Vehicle (UAV) technologies.

Hsi-Tseng Chou *et al.* (2018), investigated on the radiation characteristics of the broadband, all-metallic reflect array antennas. These antennas consisted of non-resonant convex elements for bidirectional beam applications. The metallic reflecting elements have been provided to improve the energy efficiency of these metal elements. The usage of these metallic elements improved the radiation power so as to compensate the energy lost, which occurred during prorogation in the air. These radiation characteristics exhibited, makes this antenna arrangement to radiate a broader beam. The size of the proposed antenna scheme is smaller but the gain achieved has been found to be good, resulting in better coverage. These performance metrics made this antenna system to be widely used for all wireless communication applications.

2.4 BACKGROUND STUDIES OF COMPACT CPW – FED MICROSTRIP ANTENNA SYSTEMS

Low power consumption and high speed data transfer rate features of ultra wideband technologies make them to be more suitable for wireless communication systems. The reasons for slot antennas being popular in ultra-wide bandsystems include wide frequency bandwidth, low profile, and easy integration, light weight, low cost and ease of fabrication. When the slot antennas are fed using coplanar waveguide fed mechanism, it offers low radiation leakage, low dispersion and ease of integration with active devices. Several investigators made their studies on the CPW fed antenna scheme and presented their observations and analysis. Those views have been presented as below.

Liu W C (2005) presented a novel coplanar waveguide fed planar monopole antenna using Particle Swarm Optimization (PSO) approach. This antenna arrangement has been aimed for multiband operation. The design of this antenna embeds appropriate slits into the 50 / spl Omega / feeding line, which resulted in good impedance matching for multi-resonant mode. Applying PSO algorithm the geometry parameters of the antenna have been optimized for multiband performance. The simulation and experimental setups have been devised and tested. The results obtained explored multiband operation with 10 dB impedance bandwidth of 55%, 8.5% and bandwidths of 55%, 8.5%, and 4.4% at bands of 2.51, 3.98, and 5.24 GHz, respectively. These results indicated that the system can be widely used for personal communication systems and WLAN applications. Wu C M *et al.* (2006), proposed a new non-uniform meandered and fork-type grounded antenna for triple-band WLAN applications. This antenna scheme has been proposed to meet IEE 802.11b/g/a standards. The simple and versatile design of the proposed configuration demonstrated that the radiation mechanism is clear and it could be controlled easily.

In the research studies, Costantine *et al.* (2007) presented a new design of multiband microstrip antenna for wireless communications. They presented a simple design that could be used in several band wireless operations. The range of operations include bands of GSM (880 - 960 MHz),

DCS (1710-1880 MHz), PCS (1850-1990 MHz), UMTS (1920-2170 MHz), 2.4-GHz WLAN (2400-2484 MHz), Mobile-WiMAX (IEEE 802.16e in the Taiwan: 2500-2690 MHz) and 5-GHz WLAN (5150-5350/ 5725-5825 MHz) bands. The fabricated and tested prototype provided good impedance bandwidth, radiation pattern and improved gain. A compact design T-type monopole antenna with asymmetrical ground plane for WLAN and WiMAX applications, have been addressed by Chen W S and Yu Y H (2008). This system comprises of coplanar waveguide feed antenna, using notches on the ground plane and trapezoidal feed line. These components generated broadband operation of 10 dB return loss from 1.95 GHz to 6.55 GHz. The significance of this antenna configuration is that it eliminated the undesired band. The frequency bands addressed are 2.35 GHz - 2.65 GHz, 3.28 GHz - 3.79 GHz and 5.11 GHz - 5.78 GHz. The results of the prototype exhibited good radiation characteristics with Omni-directional patterns and compact size

A small CPW-fed Triple band microstrip monopole antenna has been designed and tested by Xiaodi (2009). The design included a CPW-fed modified Sierpinski gasket monopole antenna operating at three bands as per IEEE 802.11 WLAN standards. The measured results of this arrangement indicated that the size of the antenna is compact and provided good bandwidth characteristics. The bandwidths provided by the monopole antenna are 20%, 8% and 7% for 2.45 GHz, 5.2 GHZ and 5.8 GHz respectively. These results and their corresponding analyses concluded that this scheme could be found suitable for WLAN applications. Peng Fei *et al.* (2010) planned and designed a novel CPW-fed finger-shaped antenna for ultra-wide bandapplication. The size of the proposed antenna has been of compact size the finger shaped radiator assisted to achieve S11<;-10 dB bandwidth of 2.7GHz-11GHz. The test results showed that the antenna provided Omni-directional radiation pattern, and is very suitable for short range ultra-wide bandcommunication systems.

The radiation pattern can be calculated for of a finite array from the scattering parameters between the array feeding ports. This well-known approach has been investigated by Jesus Rubio and Juan Izquierdo (2011) to make use of spherical mode expansions, by connecting with the theory of Minimum-Scattering (MS) principles. The MS theory applied estimated the radiation pattern of an array of waveguide – fed apertures. Hattan Abu Tarboush *et al.* (2011), designed a small ultra-thin Printed Inverted-F Antenna (PIFA). This antenna arrangement is capable of controlling the resonant frequencies independently. It consisted of a slotted radiator supported by shorting walls and small ground plane. These components resulted in a co pact structure and optimally operated at 2.09 GHz, 3.74 GHz and 5 GHz. The bandwidths achieved are 11%, 884% and 10% respectively, with corresponding radiation efficiencies as of 70.12%, 60.29% and 66.24%.

Ping Wang *et al.* (2012) addressed a compact CPW-fed planar monopole antenna with distinct triple bands for WiFi and WiMAX applications. This antenna provided triple band operation. It has on the edge of the radiation pattern, two I shaped notched slots and an open-ended U shaped slot. These two slots integrated symmetrical meander micro-strip lines and covered the operating bands of 2.4 GHz To 2.28 GHz, 3.27 GHz to 3.79 GHz and 5.15 GHz to 5.96 GHz. The designed antenna on testing provided excellent characteristics that include better performance interference suppression, dipole-like radiation pattern and moderate gain for WiFi and WIMAX applications. The antenna addressed by Pingan Liu *et al.* (2012) was a compact CPW-fed triple band printed antenna, which consist of a meandering split-ring slot. This antenna has been aimed for WLAN and WiMAX applications. The modified design proposed by the authors consisted of rectangular slot, with a pair of symmetrical inverted – L strips and a Y-shaped monopole radiator with a meandering split-ring slot. The fabricated antenna provided three independent frequency bands based on tuning the locations, size of the structures and three different current paths. The experimental analyses showed the independent bandwidths a 430 MHz for 2.33 GHz to 2.76 GHz, 730 MHz for 3.05 GHz to 3.88 GHz and 310 MHz for 5.57 GHz and 5.88 GHz. The return loss has been o served as less than 10 dB. A similar work has been carried out by Xu Y *et al.* (2012). The difference is that the antenna structure is modified with a rectangular ring and an S-shaped strip attached to the feed line. The bottom layer consisted of a crooked U-shaped strip and three straight strips. The simulated and experimental results are in good agreement with the communication standards by showing good impedance matching with omnidirectional radiation patterns and stable gains.

Dang Trang Nguyen *et al.* (2012) suggested a very compact printed triple band-notchedultra-wide band antenna with quarter wavelength slots. The antenna arrangement comprised to create triple band-notched characteristicsof three open-ended quarter-wavelength slots for WiMAX, WLAN and X-band satellite communication systems. The arrangement displayed a good surface current distribution patterns when tested. It also provided broad bandwidth and good omnidirectional radiation pattern in the pass-band. The key feature of this antenna scheme is that the size of the antenna designed was very compact. A square shaped microstrip antenna with Radio Frequency Identification tag (RFID) has been attempted by Horng-Dean Chen *et al.* (2012). They tried for a compact broadband dual coupling-feed circularly polarized RFID tag antenna. They mounted the tag on the metallic surface. The system has been designed for 915 MHz frequency, which is excited by a dual-offset coupling feed network with one of the feed lines a quarter-wavelength longer than the other. The selection of optimized dimensions for the coupled lines and feed-line provided appropriate impedance matching. The authors studied that the input impedance could be controlled easily by adjusting the dimensions and the implementation of dual-offset fees technique results in enhanced circularly polarized operation. The devise model provided 6 dB return loss with bandwidth of 25 MHS for 902 MHZ to 927 MHz. Correspondingly, with 3 dB axial ratio and the bandwidth has been observed as 20 MHZ for 903 MHz and 923 MHz.

Hong Chen *et al.* (2013) illustrated the working principle of triband planar monopole antenna fed with compact radiator for wireless communication systems. The design has a monopole antenna printed on the substrate with two rectangular corners cut off. The antenna has been constructed in a precise area of 3.5 x 17 mm^2, on which two inverted-L sots have been etched. This implies the three radiating elements, to produce three resonant modes of triband operations. The proposed small antenna structure had an impedance bandwidth of 10 dB of 120 MHz for the band 2.39 GHz to 2.51 GHz and 340 MHz for 3.38 GHz to 3.72 GHZ and 1450 MHz for 4.79 GHz to 6.24 GHz to cover WLAN and WiMAX applications. Naser-Moghadasi *et al.* (2013) designed a unique miniaturized dual-band coplanar waveguide – fed antenna, with a rectangular patch surrounded by upper and lower ground-plane sections. They are interconnected through a high impedance microstrip line. The size of the realized antenna had an area of 17 x 20 mm^2 and has the capability of operating at GSM and Wi-Fi and WLAN frequency bands. The experimental results of this proposed antenna arrangement exhibited monopole like radiation characteristics with a good antenna gain

Miniaturizing the size of the antenna has called for interest among many researchers. Anil Gautam *et al.* (2013) proposed a method to minimize the monopole antenna by loading inverted L-strip over the conventional monopole patch antenna. This lowered the height of the antenna. The vertical ground arrangement extended on the two sides of the radiator, effectively saved the space of the antenna. The proposed antenna design has been fabricated and tested for their performance analysis. The results portrayed that the proposed scheme had good impedance matching with constant gain and stable radiation patterns. Tero Uusitupa and Takahiro Aoyagi (2013), analyzed, the dynamic on-body communication channels for various movements and polarization schemes. The proposed study has been made through finite-difference time-domain (FDTD) method and moving human models. The human dynamical characteristics viz. walking, weakly walking and running have been considered for the design analysis. The combine effects produced nine different polarization schemes for the dipole transmitter and receiver orientations and for six receiver locations. The performance indices considered for study include reception level curves, mean levels and standard deviation of reception. The results indicated that the antenna scheme taken up for study is best applicable for electrically small dipole like antennas.

A novel reconfigurable rotated T slot antenna for cognitive radio system has been proposed by Lev Pazin and Yehuda Leviatan (2014). The antenna possesses capability of operating at any of eight adjacent sub-bands in the 6.0 GHz to 10.6 GHz frequency band. The proposed antenna consisted of eight adjacent sub-bands configure by means of seven PIN diode switches. The sub-bands provided omnidirectional radiation pattern in the horizontal plane with primarily vertical polarization. Kevin Ming-Jiang Ho and Gabriel Rebeiz *et al.* (2014) intended a microstrip antenna with frequency agility and polarization diversity. The novel feed network has been devised with Radio Frequency (RF) Micro-Electro-Mechanical Systems (MEMS) with Single Pole Double Throw (SPDT) switch. This proposed novel network provided four states of polarization control viz. linear-vertical, linear-horizontal, left-hand circular and right-handed circular polarizations. The antenna has been tuned through silicon junction tuning diodes to a center frequency from 0.9 GHZ to 1.5 GHz. The proposed antenna has been evidenced as the first of the antenna design to have four polarization states and capable of tuning a bandwidth of 1.4:1.

Adam Narbudowicz *et al.* (2015) proposed a design methodology for wideband circularly polarized slot antennas. In this design method, the slot structure employed a dual feed integrated with compact ultra-wide bandphase shifter. The design has been optimized through advanced optimization techniques and the results demonstrated that the use of spline curves generated circular polarization signals. The designed prototype evolved circular polarized bandwidth of 54% from 3.2 GHz to 6.1 GHz. In the case study done by Sabita Yadav and Saini KK (2015), the revealed that the cost of the antenna can be reduced by designing the antenna on Rogers TMM 10i substrate through dielectric constant of 10.2 and also thickness of 2.9 mm. the prosed design has resulted in a compact size with return loss of -28 dB, bandwidth of 349 MHz, gain of 11.0 dB, directivity 12.4 dBi and VSWR of 1.08. The operating frequency of the proposed system has been at 3.5 GHz. The main advantage of this antenna is that the size is compact compared to its conventional counterpart, with low making cost.

Li Ying Feng and Kwok Wa Leung (2016) in their communication investigated a new dual frequency folded parallel plate antenna with large frequency ratio. This scheme integrated the microwave parallel plate Waveguide Resonator Antenna (WRA) with millimeter-wave Fabry-Perot Resonator Antenna (FPRA). The resonant frequencies of both the antennas are independent of each other. The folded structure offered lower profile than the conventional parallel-plate WRA. The excitation of WRA part happens through a hook-shaped strip, for the FRPA it happens through L-probe with a half-ring sleeve. The proposed antenna scheme has been simulated through ANSYS HFSS and the simulated and experimental results portrayed that the radiation pattern and gain are in reasonable agreement with the each other. Mohamed Tarbouch *et al.* (2017) studied the requirements for fifth-generation (5g) wireless communication systems. They proposed a key technology to support high data transmission rate, improved signal to interference pulse noise ratio, increased spectral and energy efficiency and versatile beam shaping. They also presented the overview of the existing multibeam antenna technologies based on quasi-optical components and beam forming circuits. They studied the principles of operation, design and implementation of these technologies. They illustrated the superiority of the technologies by reviewing various application examples.

In another research work Mohamed Tarbouch *et al.* (2017 a), proposed compact CPW-fed microstrip octagonal patch antenna. This antenna scheme comprised of an H slot for WLAN and WiMAX applications. The octagonal shape has been obtained by making a cut in the four angles of the rectangular microstrip patch antenna. The addition of CPW-feed makes the antenna to possess ultra-wide bandcharacteristics. The introduction of H-slot resulted in miniaturization of the antenna, with a good impedance matching and an equitable gain. The proposed scheme has been simulated and the results have been analyzed through CADFEKO, a Method of Moment (MoM) based solver. Ka Ming Mak *et al.* (2018) presented a 5G wideband patch antenna with antisymmetric L-shaped probe feeds. The proposed design had a twin L-shaped probe feeding structure which is capable introducing feed capacitance to the antenna for broadband operation. The two L-shaped probe feeds are identical in length and feeds are antisymmetric. This design minimized the unwanted radiation and can be operated in the frequency band of 1580 MHz to 2750 MHz. this frequency range covers the current mobile systems, 3rd Generation and 4th Generation higher band frequencies. The prototype of the proposed design has been fabricated with dual slanted ±45° polarization. The simulation and experimental setups have been tested and the results have been presented. The antenna scheme suggested provided wide bandwidth of 54%

with VSWR < 2. The radiation patterns have been observed in both vertical and horizontal planes, with high isolation of -30 dB between the two input ports.

2.5 OUTCOME OF THE LITERATURE STUDIES

The literature studies depicted here elaborated the need for the compact design of antenna for GSM, Wi-Fi, and WiMAX and WLAN applications. The proposed antenna schemes should have a reasonable pass band and notched at the desired frequencies of operations. The systems should have achievable gain with less standing wave ratio. The studies implied that better performance indices can be achieved by selecting the appropriate substrate, length, height and width of the antennas and making the modification in the slots. The slots can be made in single or double layer substrates. With these inputs from the aforementioned literatures, the research work carried out with the following methodologies.

- Designing a compact microstrip line-fed ultra-wide bandantenna encompassing triple notched band
- Designing a compact single-layer triple band and microstrip line fed multifunctional patch antenna with U-slots to get multiple and wide bandwidths
- Designing a compact CPW-fed triple-band antenna

These three design system have to be studied, modeled and analyzed through suitable simulation software. The software chosen for study is Ansoft HFSS version 13.0. The prototype of the planned designs has to be fabricated and tested through Agilent's network analyzer. The proposed antenna schemes have to be evaluated for the following parameters:

Return Loss

It is the measure of low of power in the signal returned or reflected due to discontinuity in a transmission line. It is expressed in dB.

Gain

Gain is the measure of antenna's directivity and electrical efficiency.

VSWR

It is the function of reflection coefficient. It measures the power reflected from the antenna.

Radiation Pattern

It outlines the variation of power radiated by an antenna as a function of the direction away from the antenna.

2.6 CONCLUSION

Summarizing the literature, it can be stated that a good volume of research has been carried out in designing the antenna systems for Wi-Fi, WiMAX, WLAN and GSM applications. With reference to the aforesaid literature studies, in the present investigation, an attempt has been made to study the design and analysis of antenna scheme listed above. The performance of these antenna techniques taken up for study shall be critically analyzed to demonstrate the superiority of these methods.

CHAPTER 3

COMPACT TRIPLE BAND NOTCHED ULTRA-WIDE BAND ANTENNA WITH U-SLOT

3.1 INTRODUCTION

Wireless systems play a significant role in the communication field. Modern wireless systems stand in need of thoroughly incorporated Radio Frequency front-ends possessing the proficiency of multi-functional operations. In this chapter, the fundamental working principle, design, fabrication and analysis of a simple planar triple band notched ultra-wide band antenna with U-Slot has been discussed in detail. The proposed antenna system has been evaluated for its performance validation and the results have been presented.

3.2 BACKGROUND STUDIES OF ULTRA-WIDE BAND ANTENNA SCHEME

In wireless system applications, ultra-wide bandantenna design is fronting numerous encounters. One of the challenges is towards avoiding electromagnetic interfering with other prevailing narrowband service. Lee *et al.* (2012) and Naeem *et al.* (2017) suggested the use of filter to avoid the interference. However, this design leads towards larger circuit sizes and similarly increases insertion losses. Zayniyev & Budmir (2010) and Wu *et al.* (2011) specified that notched-band antennas are best examples for these filter antennas. Aragi & Vorya (2013) employed band notched ultra wide band antennas with several features/slits/bands. By transferring two C-fashioned and U-fashioned slots to patch, these antenna modeled from Yazadi & Komjani 2013 is connected with other dual-notched strands for WIMAX and WLAN frequencies. These modeled antennas retain larger sizes of 32 x 28 mm^2 and reaches out for ultra-wideband operating bands. Lu *et al.*. (2011), Wang *et al.*. 2012 and Liu *et al.*. 2013 studied and proposed a coplanar waveguide (CPW)-fed double band-notch antenna. In this antenna, the two materialized and separated band in 3.5 GHz and 5.5 GHz along with curved dual L-shaped branch is adjoined towards spherical slotted ground planes. This proposed antenna design with total dimension of 40x 30 mm^2 showsultra-wide band characteristics, and shares double notch band encompassing 3.30–3.70 gigahertz and 5.150–5.8250 GHz. Detailed analysis of ground-plane consequences in monopole antenna which is clearly described by Azim *et al.*. (2013), and the modeled ultra-wide band slot antennas has been placed over 1.6 millimeter FR4 dielectric substrates. These dual notched bands were lastly effected at 3.5 and 5.5 GHz by joining together two parasitic slits.

Liu *et al.* (2013) recommended, the notched band at 3.5 GHz, which runs zigzag was inserted into the patch and other two C-fashioned parasitic bands are surrounded at micro strip feed-line. This ends up in creating additional notched-bands concentrated in around 5.5 GHz. Consequently, this leads to the formation of small ultra-wide band antennas encompassing 3.5 or 5.5-GHz double notch bands, whose features were discussed by Chu & Yang (2008). However, the triple band-notch antenna possessing unique tri-arm resonator suggested by Jiang & Che (2012) was slightly moved to avoid interference with other two narrow bands. This ultimately exhibits better performance, but is not free from some extrinsic drawbacks which are all-encompassing the employment of several filter essentials, employment of large spaces in antennas, and also stronger connection among these filtering components.

From all these related works, it is evident how a compact microstrip line-fed ultra-wide bandantennas incorporating triple notched band has been investigated, thereby fabricated. It encompasses one tri-arm resonator behind the substrate and a U-slot on the radiator surface. This antenna can be operated in three different modes in order to cover frequency bands of Wi-Max, WLAN and X-band satellite communications. This designed antenna is smaller in size and exhibits better radiation performance when compared with the prevailing schemes.

3.3 ULTRA-WIDE BAND ANTENNA

Ultra wide-band is a radio technology it uses very low energy level for short-range, high-bandwidth communications. It covers a large portion of the radio spectrum. Ultra-wide band differs from spread spectrum as it transmits such that the waves don't interfere with conventional narrowband and carrier wave transmission in the same frequency band. Ultra-wide band transmits information over a large bandwidth of more than 500 MHz. The applications of Ultra-wide band include data collection, non-cooperative radar imaging, precision locating and tracking applications.

3.3.1 Features of ULTRA-WIDE BAND Antenna

Ultra-wide band transmits information by generating radio energy at specific intervals and occupies a large bandwidth. In this way, it enables pulse-position or time modulation. The conventional radio transmissions transmit information by varying the power level, frequency and phase of a sinusoidal wave. This is the difference between conventional and ultra-wide bandradio schemes. ultra-wide bandpermits modulation of the information by encoding the polarity of the pulse, its amplitude or by using orthogonal pulses. These ultra-wide bandpulses can be sent sporadically or rates up to the inverse of the ultra-wide bandpulse bandwidth. The channel pulse rates supported include 1.3 giga pulses per second. It supports forward error correction encoded data rates in excess of 675 Mbits/s.

The key aspect of ultra-wide bandtechnology is its ability to determine the "Time of Flight", of the transmission at various frequencies, which helps to overcome the multipath propagation. The distances can be measured using cooperative symmetric two-way metering technique. This results in high resolution and accuracy, by compensating for local drift and stochastic inaccuracy. The pulses of ultra-wide bandare very short. They are less than 60 cm for a 500 MHz- wide pulse and less than 23 cm for a 1.3 GHz-bandwidth pulse. These pulses make the signal reflections not to overlap with the original pulse and so there is no multipath fading of narrow signals. This is an important feature of ultra-wide bandantennas. If there is any multipath propagation and inter-pulse propagation, it can be mitigated though coding techniques.

3.4 ULTRA-WIDE BAND NOTHCED BAND ANTENNAS

The commercial applications of ultra-wide band spectrum came into existence since 2002. These systems operate in such a wide frequency band and low power emission level. It could be easily interfered by the nearby communication systems. These interference signals could be suppressed by using Radio Frequency (RF) filtering. The drawback of traditional filtering is that the usage of lumped elements increases the cost, system complexity and occupies more space. This problem could be overcome by designing the ultra-wide band antennas with band-notched characteristics to suppress the interference signals. Figure 3.1 illustrates the design concept of ultra-wide bandnotched band antenna.

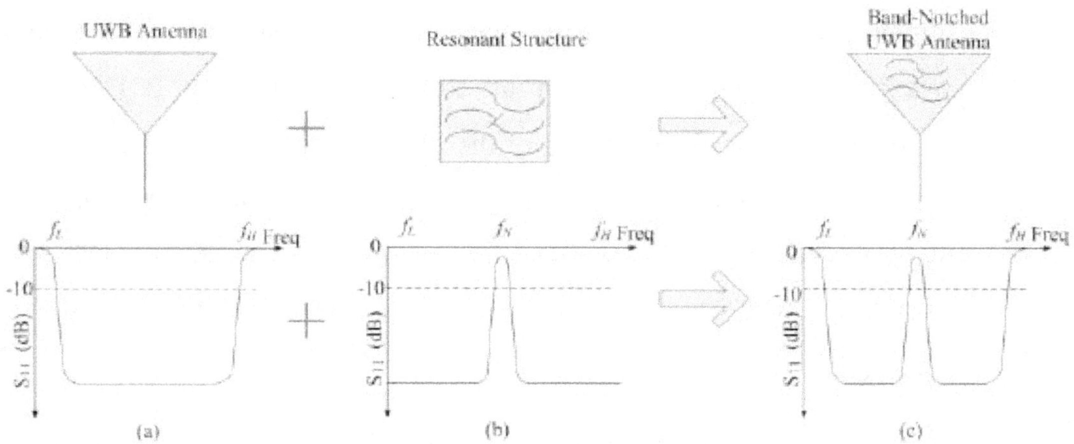

Figure 3.1 Design Concept of ultra-wide bandNotched Band Antenna

The ultra-wide bandantenna treated with a resonant structure results in ultra-wide bandBand notched antenna. The impedance bandwidth of it ranges from f_L to f_H, which are the lowest and highest 10-dB cut-off frequencies respectively. f_N is the resonant frequency of the band stop resonant structure. Combining these two structures gives ultra-wide bandband-notched antenna. The antenna resulted will not interfere with the other communication systems, that have the frequency band as f_N. The notches are created in antennas to ensure that the ultra-wide bandsignal doesn't affect the allotted spectral ranges for various applications.

In general, ultra-wide bandantenna operates in the frequency range of 3.1 to 10.6 GHz. The band notch characteristics aids the ultra-wide band antenna to avoid interference with co-existing band like Wi-MAX band the lower WLAN band (5.15-5.35 GHz), and higher WLAN band (5.725–5.875 GHz), and X-band downlink satellite communication (7.1-7.76 GHz).

3.5 BLOCK DIAGRAM OF PROPOSED ULTRA-WIDE BAND ANTENNA

The block diagram of the proposed antenna scheme implementation is portrayed in Figure 3.2. The first block defines the design specification of antenna such as Relative permittivity (ε_r) of substrate, Resonance frequency f_r, Height of the antenna substrate (h). The second block defines the design calculation of Width and Length of the antenna. The third block defines the software design of antenna by using Ansoft HFSS version 13.0. Then the antenna is simulated and the results of the antenna have been analyzed.

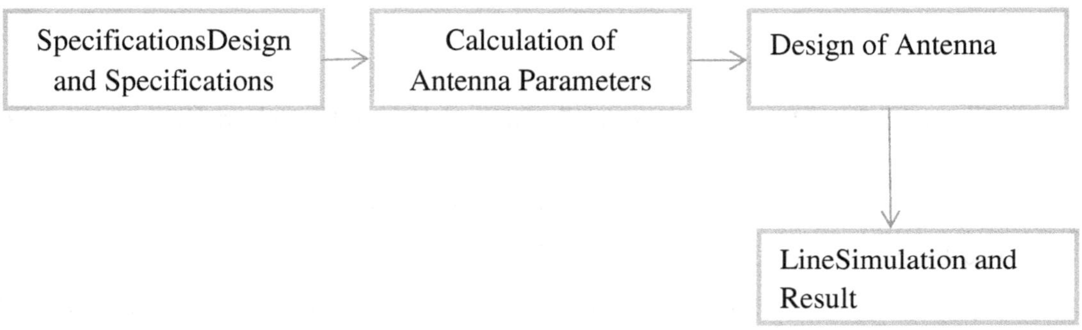

Figure 3.2 Block Diagram of Antenna Design

The design includes selection of appropriate dielectric constant of the substrate (ε_r), the resonant frequency (f_r), and the height of the substrate h. The design procedure involves the following steps:

Step 1: Specify

- Dielectric constant of the Substrate (ε_r)
- Resonant frequency of the antenna (f_r)
- Height of the Substrate (h)

Step 2: Determine

- Width of the Patch (W)

- Length of the Patch (L)

3.5.1 Design Specifications

(a) Dielectric Constant of the substrate

There are numerous substrates that can be used for the design of microstrip antennas, and their dielectric constants are usually in the range of $2.2 \leq \varepsilon_r \leq 12$. Usually, thick substrates with lower dielectric constants are chosen owing to their better efficiency, larger bandwidth and loosely bound field surface for radiation into the space. The main drawback of thick substrate is that the cost of the substrate increases with increase in thickness. On the other hand, thinner substrates with higher dielectric constants found suitable for microwave circuits. They require tightly bound fields to minimize undesired radiation and coupling. This leads to decrease in the size of the substrate. Their disadvantages include increased losses, less efficiency and smaller bandwidths. Due to these factors, the dielectric constant for the FR4 substrate is chosen as given in Equation 3.1.

$$\varepsilon_r = 4.6 \tag{3.1}$$

(b) Resonant Frequency:

The Resonant frequency of the desired antenna scheme is chosen as in Equation 3.2,

$$f_r = 5.3 \text{ GHz} \tag{3.2}$$

(c) Height of the substrate:

The height of the substrate is selected as in Equation 3.3,

$$h = 1.6\text{mm} \tag{3.3}$$

From the aforementioned design considerations, the length and width of the desired antenna structure has been evaluated as W_s = 29mm and

L_s = 20.5mm.The length of the microstrip transmission line is determined using Equation 3.4.

$$TL=\lambda/4=\lambda_0/4\sqrt{\varepsilon r} \tag{3.4}$$

Where,

$\lambda_0 = c/f_0$ =.1, f_0 = 5.3GHz, ε_r=4.6, c=3.00e+008 m/s.

3.6 GEOMETRY OF PROPOSED ULTRA-WIDE BAND ANTENNA

The geometry of the planned antenna configuration is depicted in Figure. 3.3. It consists of a microstrip line-fed antenna with a U-slot etched on the surface of the radiator. The length and width of the tri-arm resonator has been modified to obtain the triple notched bands.

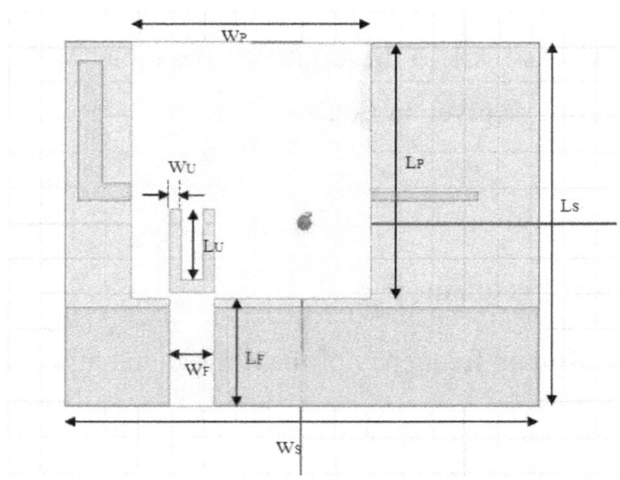

Figure 3.3 Geometry of triple band antenna

3.7 DESIGN AND OPTIMIZATION OF PROPOSED ANTENNA

In this research work, a compact triple band notched ultra-wide band antenna with U-Slot has been proposed. The proposed antenna scheme encompasses a rectangular patch of 14.5 × 14.75 mm^2 on double-sided 1.6-millimeter thickness FR-4 Printed Circuit Board (PCB). This substrate material comprises of dielectric constant 4.6, with loss tangent as 0.02. The side length from ground plane is 5.5 mm and is etched out on the side as shown in Figure 3.3. The patch of the antenna is connected forcibly in the conducting part of the ground planes. This enables the modeled scheme to work efficiently, while associating diverse resonance governing towards wider operating bands as proposed by Azimet and Haroom (2014). This antenna has a compact profile of 20.5 × 29 mm^2, the antenna's operating band being sufficient to shelter frequency bands of 3.1 gigahertz to 10.6 gigahertz. For generating triple-notched band towards WiMAX, WLAN and X band satellite communications, the tri-arm resonators are imprinted over the ground planes and U-fashioned slit is created inner to the radiator surface as illustrated in Figure 3.4.

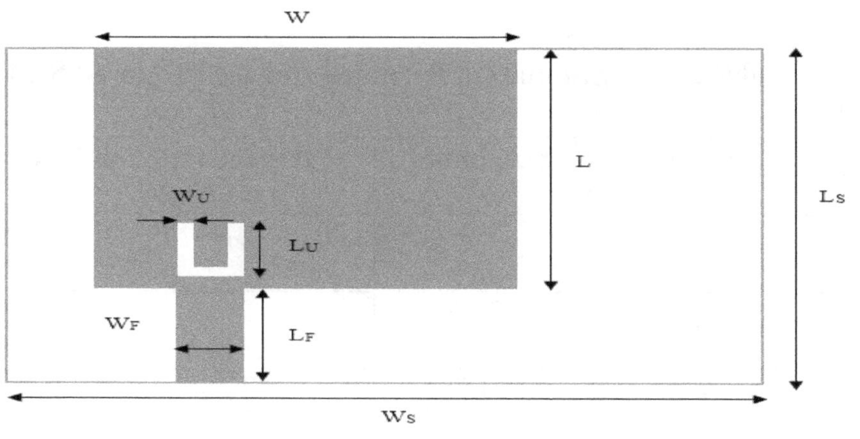

(a) Upper Layer

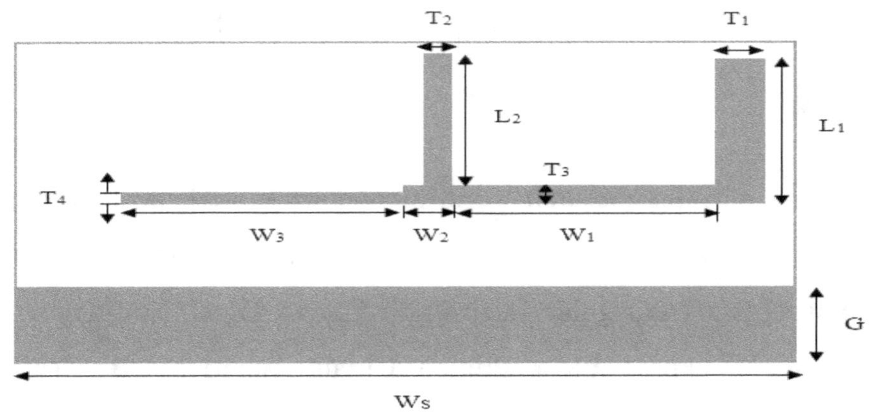

(b) Lower Layer

Figure 3.4 Articulation of Antenna Structure

Additional spaces are not mandatory for inserting the parasitic resonator and U-slot. This makes the overall extent of antennas to remain identical. By modifying these resonator parameters and adding additional slot into the radiator surface, the triple notched bands could be achieved. This designed antenna is excited by the use of microstrip line feed. The design parameters towards anticipated antennas have been described in Table 3.1. These parameters have been optimized using finite element method with commercially available Ansoft HFSS 12 Software. The lengths and widths of the U-Slot and notch frequencies are varied to study the performance analysis. The results are tabulated as in Table 3.2.

Table 3.1 Simulation Parameter of the Proposed Scheme

Parameter	Size in mm	Parameter	Size in mm
W_S	29	L_1	8
L_S	20.5	L_2	6.77
W	14.75	T_1	1.5
L	14.5	T_2	0.9

W_U	0.7	T_3	1
L_U	4.7	T_4	0.5
W_F	2.8	W_1	11
L_F	6	W_2	1.5
G	6	W_3	10.5

Table 3.2 Gain Disparity as a function of L_U and W_U

L_U (mm)	Gain (dBi)	W_U (mm)	Gain (dBi)
3	4.25	0.5	2.8
4	4.6	0.6	4.4
4.7	5.0	0.7	4.9
5	4.6	0.8	4.1

3.8 EXPERIMENTAL RESULTS AND DISCUSSIONS

The performance study begins with the construction of the proposed antenna begins with the following design considerations:

(i) An antenna which has only patch and ground plane and it can be operated over 3.1 to 10.6 GHz. By adding tri-arm resonator at the back of substrate as in Antenna.

(ii) An antenna that can be made to work as dual band-notched one.

(iii) An antenna with an additional U-slot that has been created into the patch. Therefore, it can be operated as triple band-notched antenna.

The aforementioned antenna schemes have been simulated and the corresponding results have been analyzed and presented in Figure 3.4. The top layer is illustrated in Figure 3.5 (a) and the bottom layer is viewed in Figure 3.5(b).

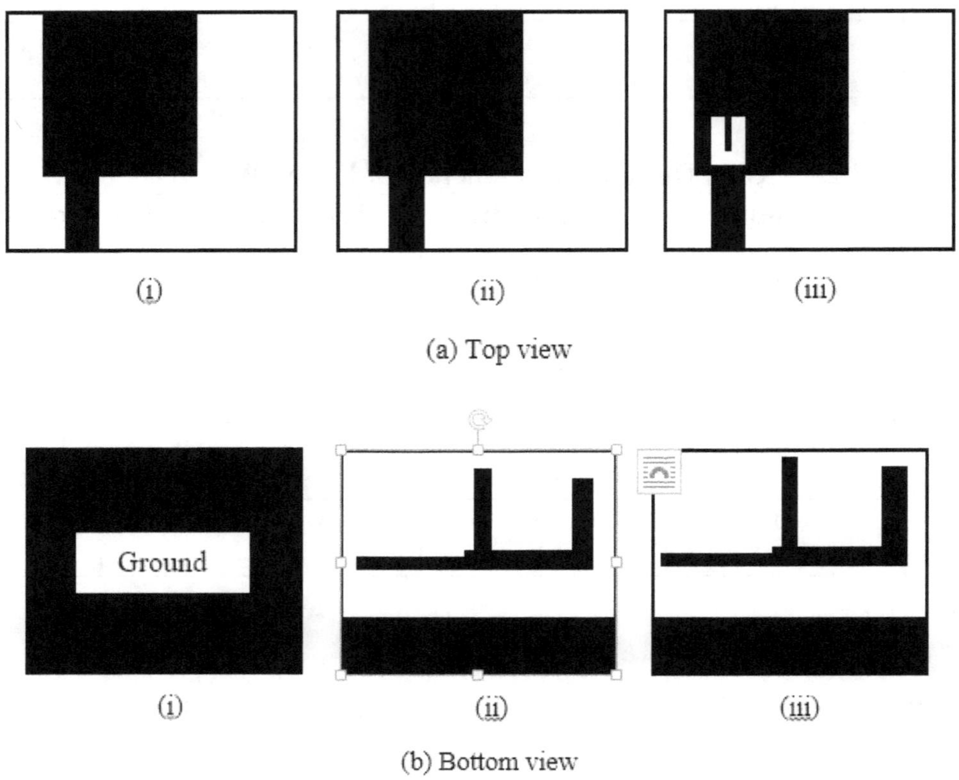

Figure 3.5 Arrangement of the Prospective Scheme

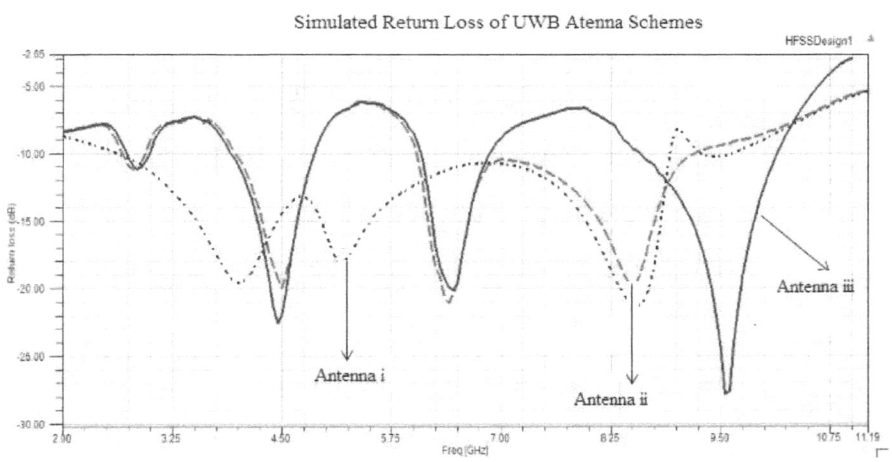

Figure 3.6 Simulated Antenna Losses

The evaluation of the proposed schemes and the simulated return losses have been entailed in Figure 3.6. From the return losses and the gain disparity tabulated in Table 3.2, it is evidenced that the antenna (i) is a ultra-wide bandantenna which is operated over the complete frequencies of 3.10 gigahertz - 10.60 gigahertz. Antenna (ii) provides dual-notch band encompassing center-frequencies around 3.50 gigahertz and 5.50 gigahertz. The proposed scheme (iii) gives an additional notched band which is operated at 8.2 gigahertz. With these results, it is inferred that the antenna design scheme which has additional notched band is a triple band notched antenna and it's the optimized design. Therefore the further analyses have been made only on this proposed triple band notched antenna scheme only.

From the optimized design, of the proposed antenna scheme, the surface current delivery has been observed. Figure 3.7 portrays the surface currents in triple notch band ultra-wide bandantennas for 3.5 Gigahertz. It shows that, the surface current in the antenna is focused powerfully at the resonator and slot. Current flows in a direction ambiguous towards the radiating patches. Consequently, results in weaker effective radiations. Resonator leads to extra path for surface current, thereby at notch frequency, this surface current at resonator is ambiguous towards radiator current. Therefore, at notch frequency, this surface current is suggestively trimmed down, ensuing towards the creation of triple-notched band.

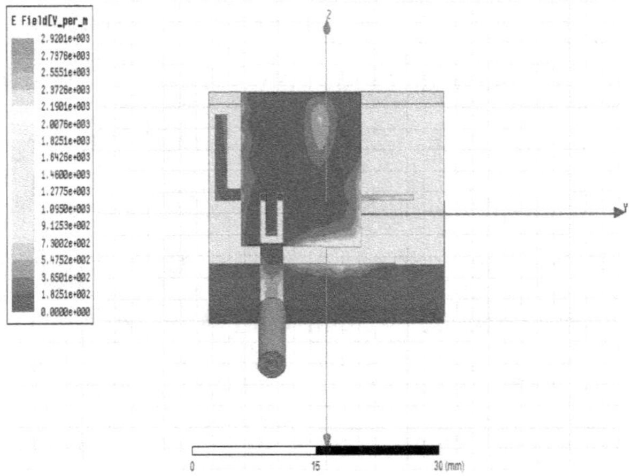

Figure 3.7 Surface Current

The return losses of the prospective band-notch antennas encompassing parasitic resonator with U-slot is displayed in Figure 3.8. In comparison with the antenna deprived of filter elements, it becomes evident that the input impedances are not matched with the 50-Ω characteristic impedances, therefore leading to incongruity towards the notch frequency.

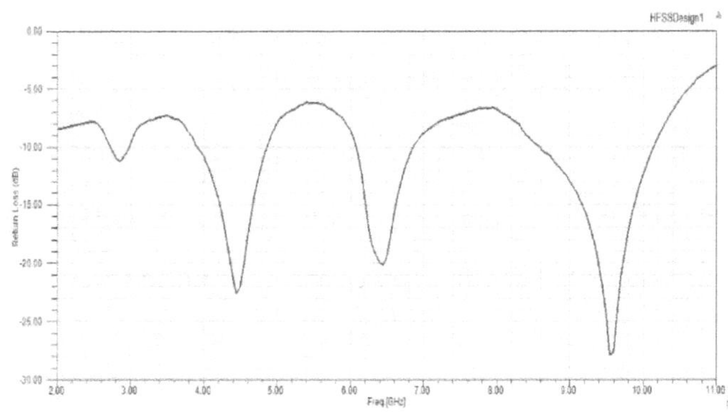

Figure 3.8 Return Loss of the Prospective Approach

Radiation pattern of prospective scheme encompassing 3.5 gigahertz, 6.5 gigahertz and 10.2 gigahertz for E and H planes were exhibited in Figure 3.9. The proposed scheme clearly displays Omni-directional radiation pattern at E and H-planes. Moreover, there becomes evidence that, in comparison with radiation pattern at pass-band frequency around 6.5 gigahertz and 10.2 gigahertz, and in 3.5 gigahertz (notched band) gain has been quenched up suggestively in every direction.

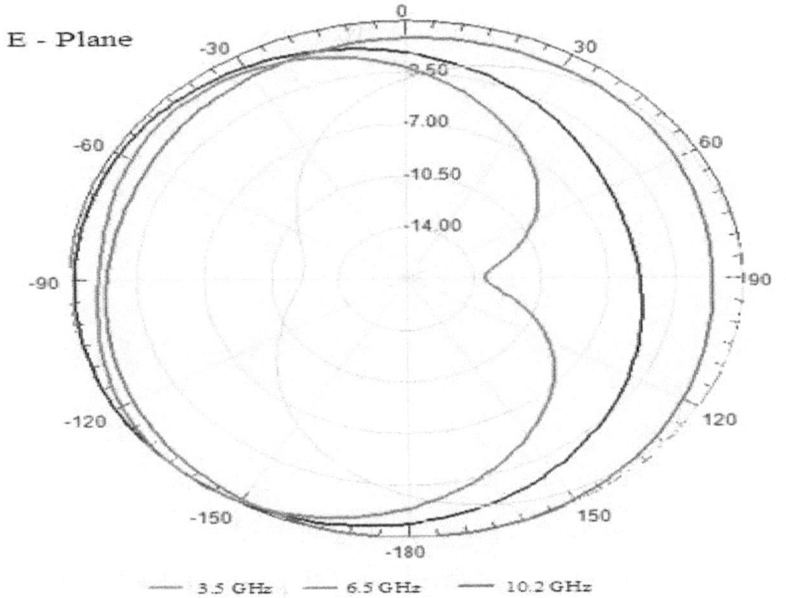

(a) E-Plane

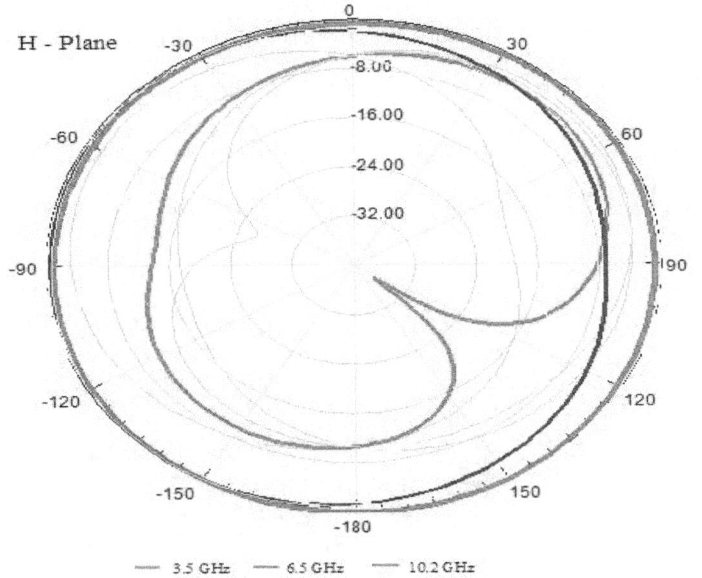

(b) H – Plane

Figure 3.9 Radiation Pattern

Figure 3.10 entails simulation results of peak gain plot targeting this prototyped approach. It could be concluded that, the proposed scheme displays excellent gain over complete operating bands, excluding radical decrease in notched band. This antenna could achieve more than 5 dBi around pass band frequencies, and nearly 0 dBi at notch band frequencies.

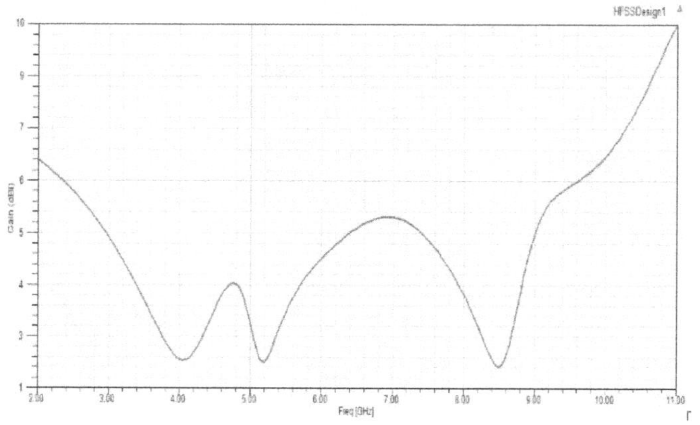

Figure 3.10 Gain of the proposed scheme

Figure 3.11 enumerates fabricated antenna and pictures that, this realized antenna is smaller in size, thereby shows good radiation excluding the notched band. Being tested by N9926A vector network analyzer (VNA), results of this contrived antenna is pinpointed at 4.5 gigahertz, 5.5 gigahertz and 8.2 gigahertz that are roughly same as the simulated results.

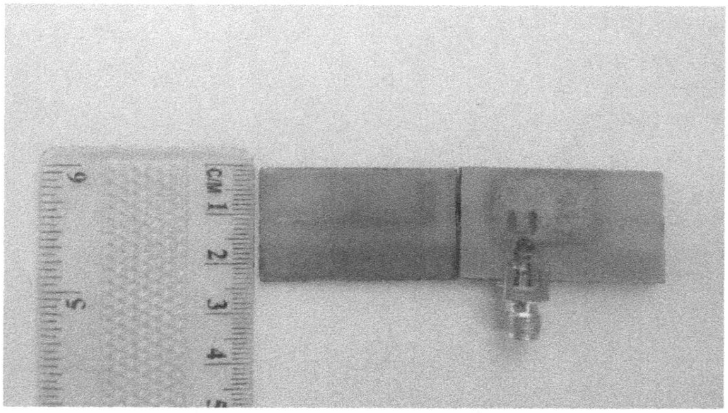

Figure 3.11 Portrait of Fabricated Triple Notched Band ULTRA-WIDE BAND Scheme

The simulated and measured values of the return losses are shown in Figure 3.12. The results infer that the both the loss outcomes are very-well matched, so that this prototyped antenna could be suited for WiMAX pinpointed in 3.5 gigahertz, WLAN pinpointed in 5.5 gigahertz and X-Band satellite communication services for downlink purpose pinpointed in 8.2 gigahertz.

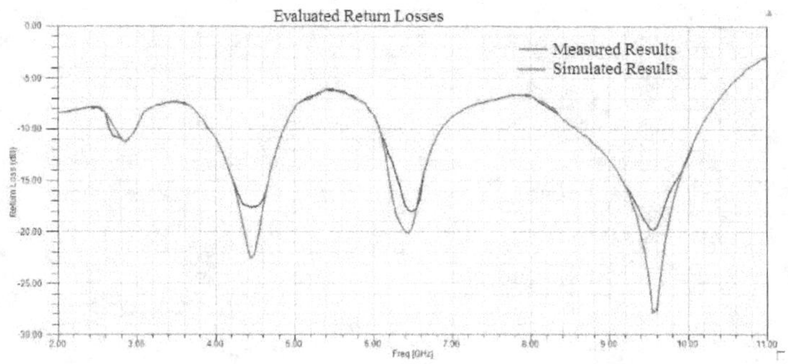

Figure 3.12 Evaluated Return Loss Curve

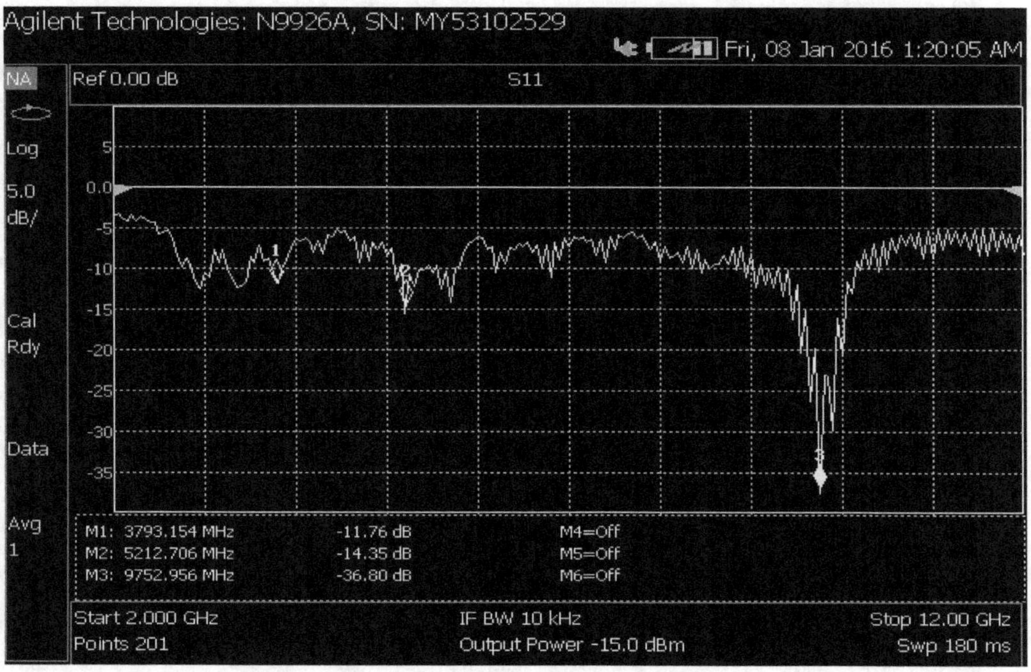

(a) Return Loss

(b) Standing Wave Ratio

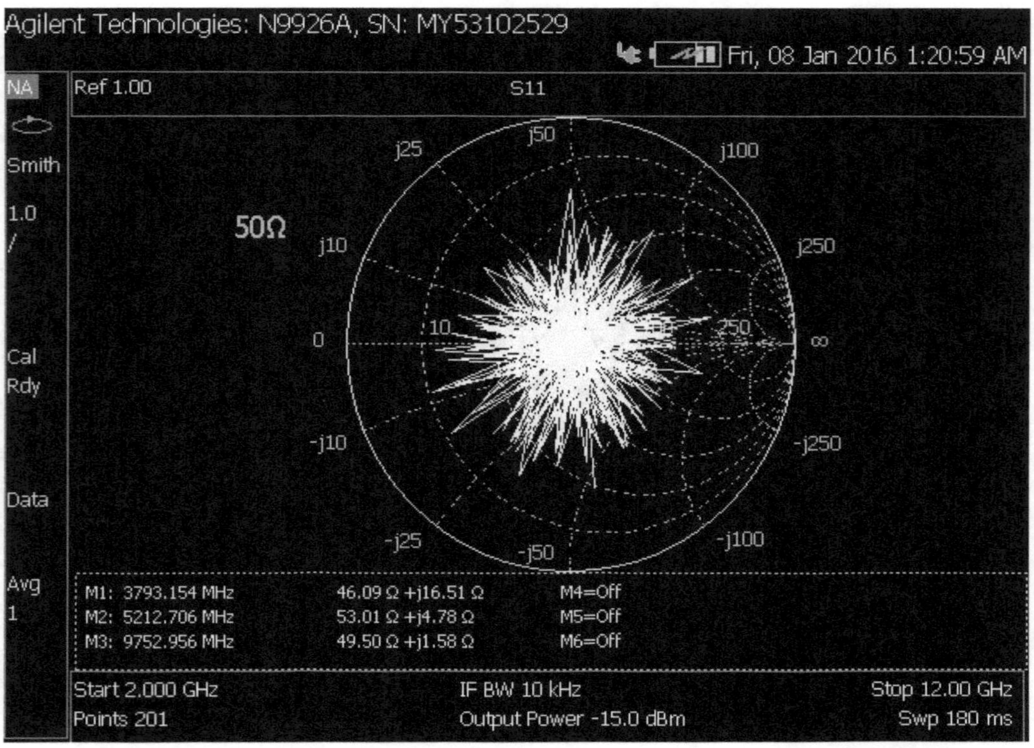

(c) Smith Chart Analysis

Figure 3.13 Results from Network Analyzer

The prototype model of the proposed antenna configuration has been tested with Agilent's Network Analyzer. The results have been depicted in Figure 3.13. The return loss measured from network analyzer has been depicted in Figure 3.13 (a). The voltage standing wave ratio and the smith chart response analysis have been displayed in Figure 3.13 (b) and 3.13 (c) respectively. These results infer that the proposed scheme of compact single triple band notched ultra-wide bandantenna with single U-slot provides operating bands are 3.5 GHz, 5.5 GHz and 8.2 GHz. The voltage standing wave ratio has also been found to be less than 2, with a gain of 5.2 dBi. The pass bandwidth has been observed as 62%.

Table 3.3 Comparative Analysis

Parameter	Existing Antenna	Proposed Antenna
Notched bands	Two (at 3.5, 5.5 GHz)	Three (at 3.5, 5.5, 8.2 GHz)
Gain	4.4 dBi	5.2 dBi
VSWR	< 2	<2
Pass bandwidth	83%	62%

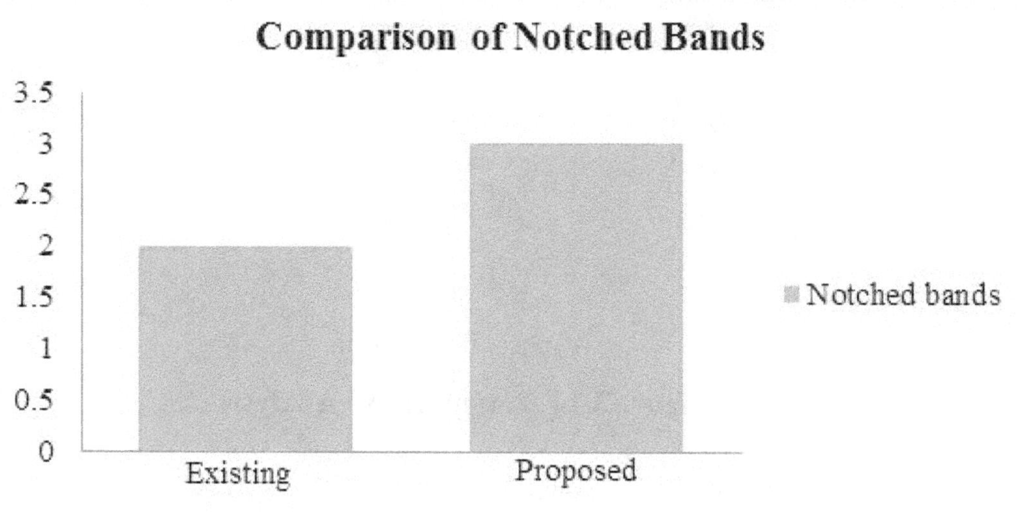

(a) Notched Bands

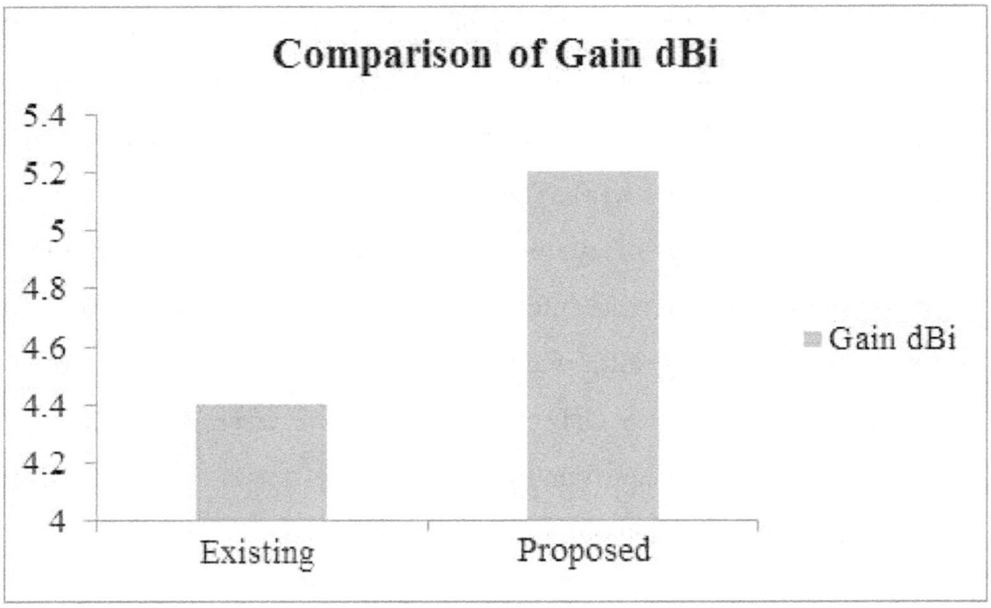

(b) Gain

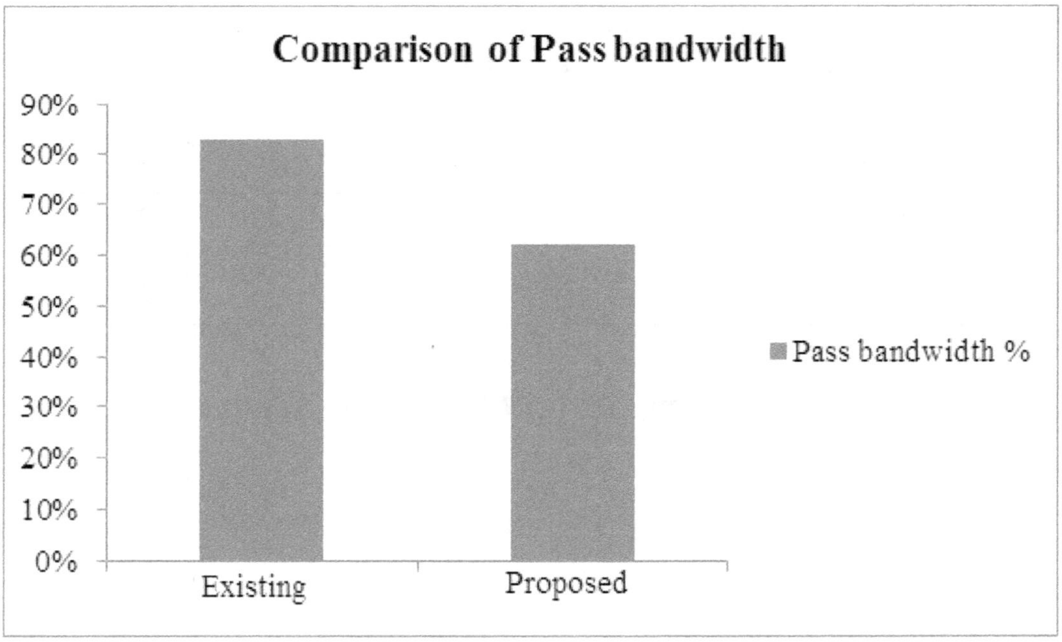

(c) Pass Bandwidth

Figure 3.14 Comparative Analysis

A comparative study has been made with the existing antenna scheme and the proposed antenna design scheme. The performance parameters taken up for the study and their values estimated have been tabulated in Table

3.3. Figure 3.14 (a) illustrates the comparison of notched bands of existing and proposed antenna system. Figure 3.14 (b) depicts the comparison of gain and Figure 3.14 (c) shows the comparison of pass bandwidth of the existing and proposed scheme of interest. The prospective design possesses better performance towards gain, radiation pattern and return loss over complete operational frequency ranges. The notched bands of the existing antenna schemes are only two i.e. at 3.5 and 5.5 GHz, whereas the proposed optimized design has been resulted in three notched bands viz. 3.5, 5.5 and 8.2 GHz frequencies. The gain of the proposed antenna scheme is 5.2 dBi which is higher compared to the existing scheme, which has only 4.4 GHz. The pass bandwidth of the proposed scheme is 62%, which is superior to the existing scheme.

3.9 CONCLUSION

A simple planar triple band-notch antenna has been designed and evaluated towards ultra wide band usages. The triple notched band at 3.5 gigahertz, 5.5 gigahertz and 8.2 gigahertz for the narrow band state ($|S_{11}| \leq -10$ dB) has been created. The design has been modified such that the proposed scheme has combined underneath radiating element and U-slot etched to it at the radiator surface.

The proposed antenna scheme has been simulated and results have been tabulated. The experimental studies and the corresponding results are tabulated. The optimized design resulted in the rejection of frequency bands at essential inquisitive frequencies. This validated the proposed design as it resulted in better harmonic suppressions encompassing manageable pass band bandwidth of 62% using slot and resonator. The proposed antenna scheme resulted in a higher gain of 5.2%. The proposed antenna scheme when tested with Agilent's network analyzer implies the similar results of this simulation model. The comparative analysis made between the existing and proposed antenna schemes, inferred that the proposed scheme provides superior performance as mentioned earlier in all aspects of the performance parameters, than the existing antenna schemes.

Thus, these compact triple notched band ultra-wide bandantennas could be observed to be a suitable aspirant towards wireless communication system. The proposed antenna scheme has been aimed towards averting interferences with WiMAX, WLAN and X- band satellite communication (downlink) services towards ultra-wideband.

CHAPTER 4

TRIPLE BAND ULTRA-WIDE BAND ANTENNA WITH DOUBLE U-SLOT

4.1 INTRODUCTION

The sweeping expansion in the field of wireless communicationshas resulted huge demand for multi-band antennas. In single communication systems, multi-band antenna plays a vital role to meet the communication standards. The efficient features of planar antennas viz. simple structure, compactness and low manufacturing cost, makes them suitable for various applications like GSM, Wi-Fi and WiMAX. In these antennas, U-Slots are employed mainly to enhance the bandwidth, rather than introducing notched band. The significance usage of U-slot is that it enables multi-band characteristics. Designing antennas for GSM, WLAN and WiMAX applications becomes more tedious, as they employ bands operating at several frequency ranges. In this Chapter, a single compact triple-band antenna with double U-slot has been attempted. The design, analysis, simulation model and results have been presented. The aimed antenna scheme has been simulated using Ansoft HFSS version 13.0.

4.2 MULTILAYER PATCH ANTENNA

As mentioned earlier, the design of multi-band microstrip patch antenna that too with narrow band width is a challenging task. The patch antennas should be properly designed with strips or slots to achieve the desired band of operations. The cost of the patch increases, when the bandwidth increases, as because increasing the bandwidth needs the improvement in impedance of the antenna. In this aspect, the multilayer patch structure enhances the impedance and possesses the same characteristics over operating frequency band. Low dielectric constant materials are being used to realize the multilayer microstrip antenna. These substrates improve the impedance making the antenna to be widely used for broadband applications. In order to achieve multiple resonant frequencies, the air gap length has to be increased. The resonant behavior offered by the antenna scheme can be considered as a coupling between two resonating modes in the dielectric regions through the air gap.

4.3 DESIGN OF TRIPLE-LAYER DOUBLE U-SLOT PATCH ANTENNA

Researchers have suggested many techniques to design microstrip patch antenna with multiband characteristics. The designs reported by them introduces multilayer via incorporating slots or strips. The same methodology has been adopted in this research work. The design incorporates a combination of dual U-slot and multiple layers to achieve multiple bands and wide bandwidth. This research work proposes a multiband triple-layer probe fed double U-slot microstrip patch antennas. The design geometry of the proposed and designed fabricated antenna structure has been described in Figure 41 and antenna of the top layer of the proposed antenna is portrayed in Figure 4.1 (a) and the side view in Figure 4.1 (b). The design parameters have been tabulated in Table 4.1.

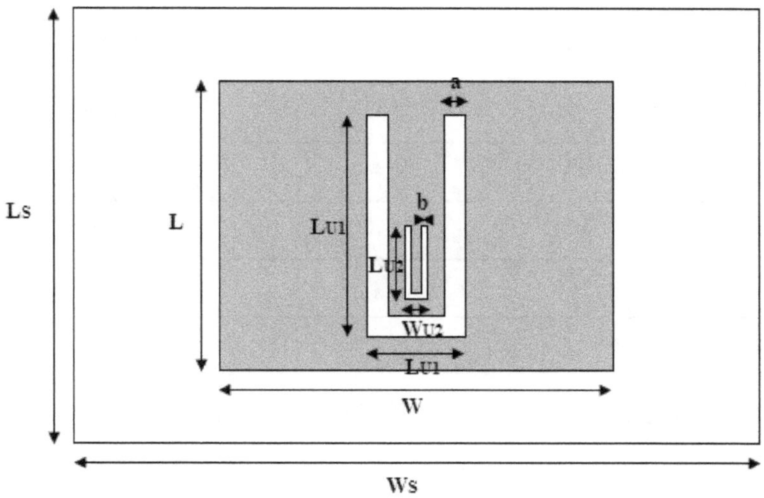

(a) Top Layer

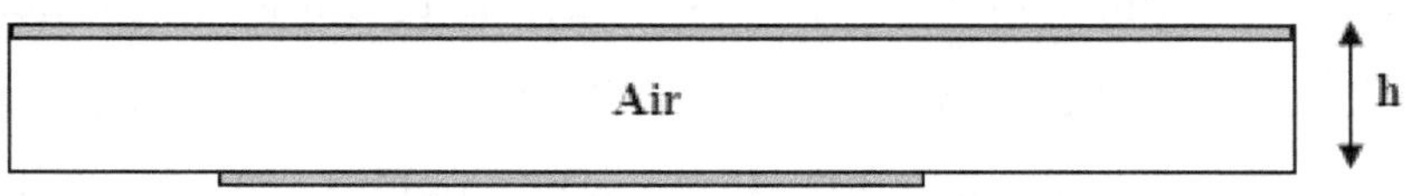

Figure 4.1(b) Side view

Figure 4.1 Geometry of Triple layer patch Antenna

Table 4.1 Design Parameters of Triple layer patch Antenna

PARAMETERS	SIZE (mm)
L_S	124.00
W_S	78.500
L	71.000
W	52.000
L_{U1}	40.00
W_{U1}	18.000
L_{U2}	13.000

W_{U2}	4.000
A	4.000
B	1.000
H	11.700
L_G	78.500
W_G	78.500

4.3.1 Design of Multi-band Patch Antenna

The design of the proposed antenna configuration is depicted in Figure 4.2. In this design, a coaxial line-fed microstrip patch antenna with a dimension of 71 x 52 mm^2 has been etched on one side of a top FR4 substrate material. The ground plane with length L_G and width W_G is etched on the bottom layer. The dielectric constant of the substrate employed is 4.4 and the loss tangent of the same is 0.002. The patch is fed by a 50 Ω coaxial line. The patch and the ground plane has 8.5mm gap between of them . The 3-D view of the proposed antenna design is portrayed in Figure 4.2.

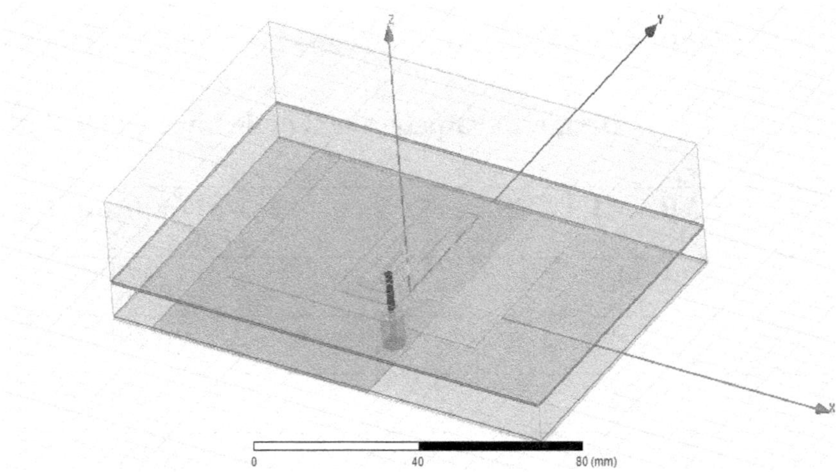

Figure 4.2 3-D view of Proposed Antenna Scheme

The figure 4.2 illustrates that the size of the proposed antenna scheme is relatively small and hence it becomes a small multiband microstrip patch antenna. This proposed antenna is capable of operating at three different frequencies viz. 1.6 GHz, 1.9 GHz and 3.8 GHz, when the substrate thickness is 1.6 mm.

4.4 SIMULATIONAL ANALYSIS

The proposed single layer triple band microstrip patch antenna has been simulated using Ansoft HFSS Version 13.0. The simulation results and the corresponding discussions are presented in the following sections.

4.4.1 Results and Discussions

A solution type is Driven Terminal because it gives solutions in terms of voltages and current while Driven Modal uses power. An air box is created around the antenna structure. The air box has to be created in to model open space so that the radiation from the antenna's structure is absorbed and not reflected back towards the radiator. It should be a quarter-wavelength long of the operating frequency of interest.

The return loss measured from the simulation loss is shown in Figure 4.3. Figure 4.3 (a) exhibits the return loss for 1.6 mm substrate. It illustrates that the operating bands are 1.6 gigahertz, 1.9 gigahertz and 3.8 gigahertz, for a substrate thickens of 1.6 mm. When the thickness is reduced to 0.6 mm, the operating bands exhibited are 1.8 gigahertz, 2.2 gigahertz and 4.8 gigahertz. It is evident from Figure 4.3 (b) that shows the return loss of 0.6 mm substrate.

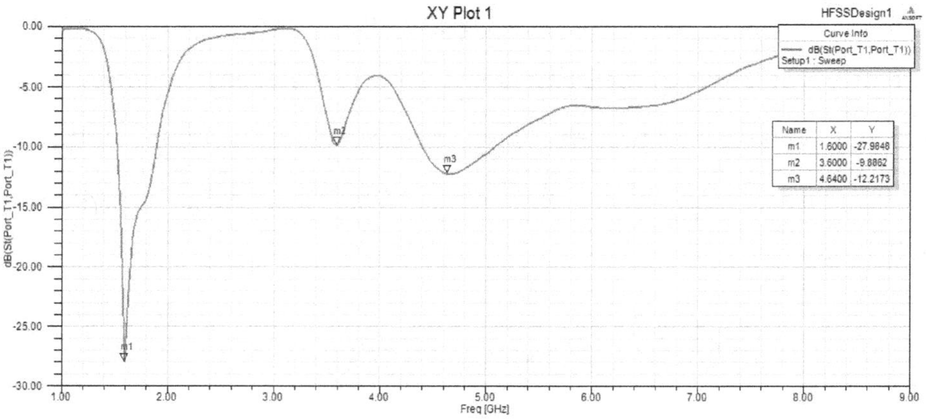

(a) 1.6 mm

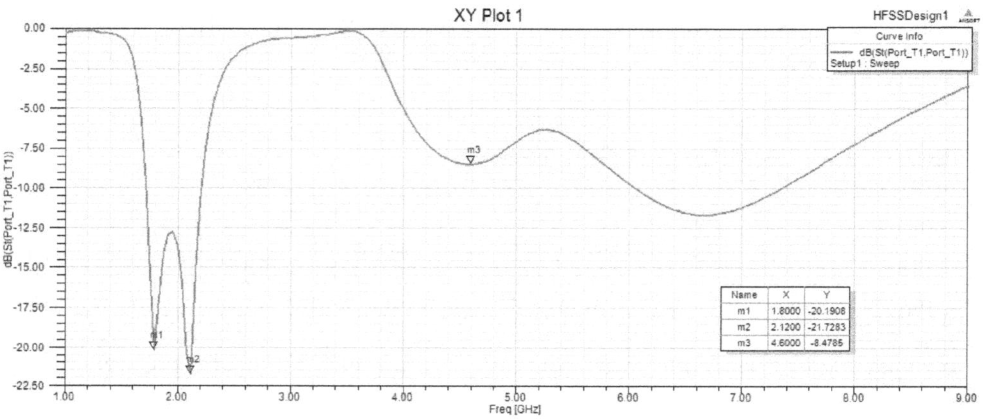

(b) 0.6 mm

Figure 4.3 Simulated Return Losses

The Voltage Standing Wave Ratio (VSWR) of the proposed antenna configuration simulated for the thickness of 1.6 GHz, 1.9 GHz and 3.8 GHz, has been displayed in Figure 4.4. The VSWR plot exemplifies that the antenna provides VSWR less than 2 at all desired frequency bands. This illustrates that the 1.6 mm substrate achieves a bandwidth of 400 MHz, whereas the substrate with 0.6 mm has bandwidth of 600 MHz.

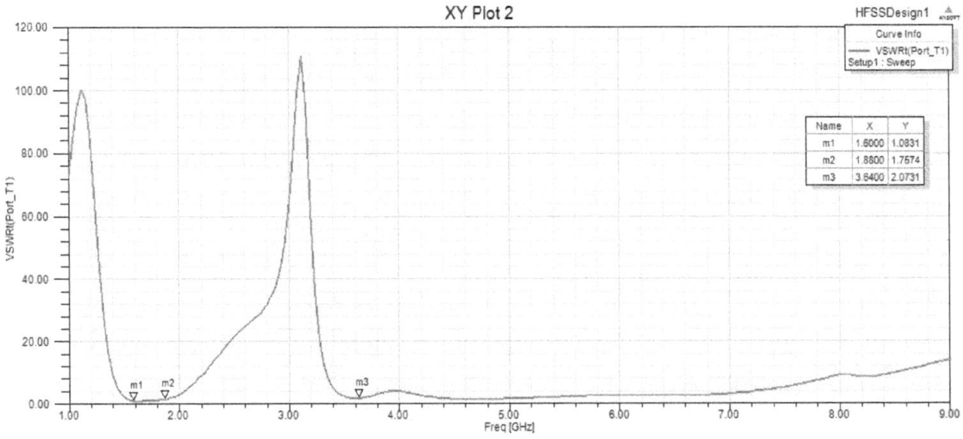

Figure 4.4 Simulated VSWR

Table 4.2 Comparative Analysis

Parameter	Existing Antenna	Proposed Antenna
Notched bands	2	3
Gain	4.4 dBi	4.8 dBi
VSWR	< 2	< 2
Pass bandwidth	83%	73%

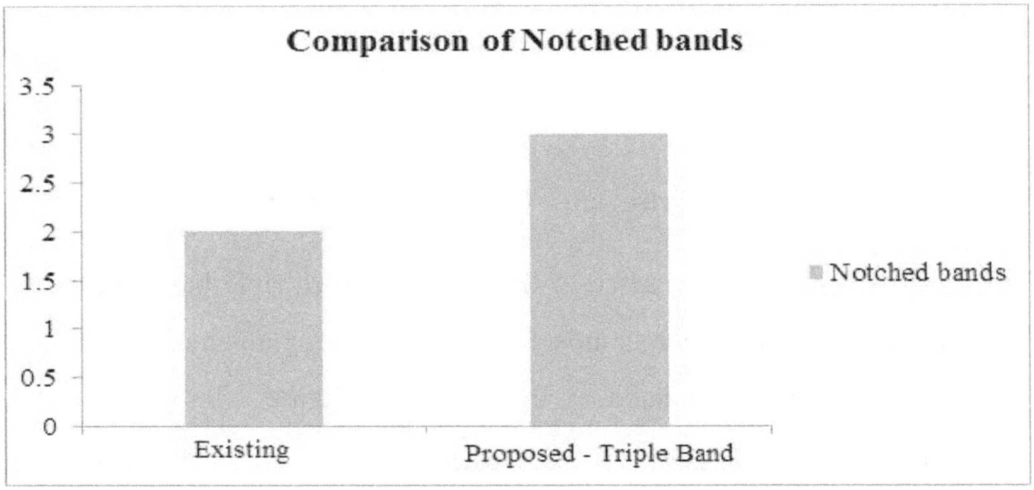

(a) Notched Bands

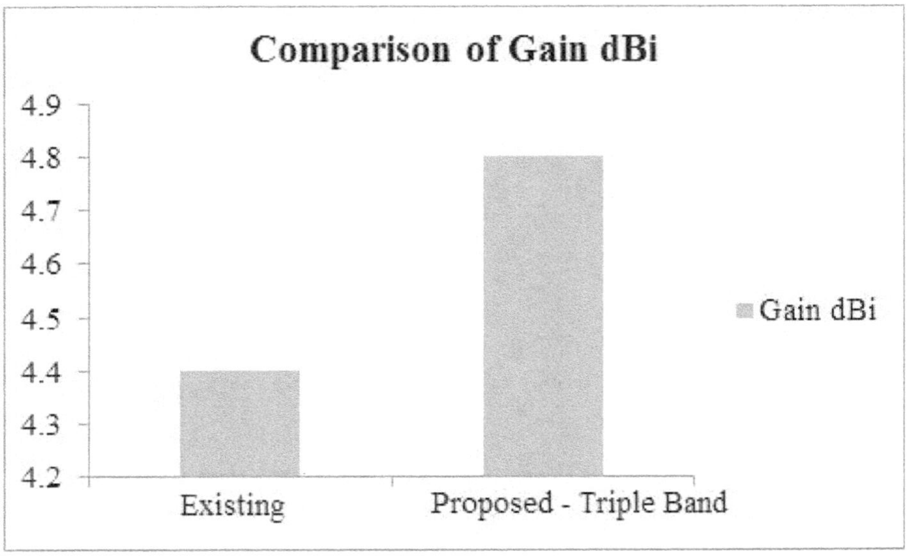

(b) Gain

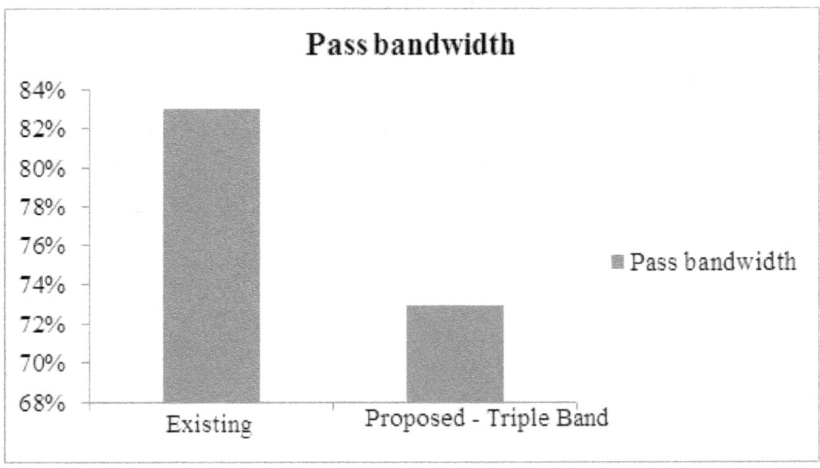

(c) Pass Bandwidth

Figure 4.5 Comparative Analysis

The performance of the recommended triple band double U-slot antenna scheme has been compared with the existing antenna scheme and the results have been tabulated as in Table 4.2. Figure 4.5 (a) illustrates the comparison of notched bands of existing and proposed antenna system. Figure 4.5 (b) depicts the comparison of gain and Figure 4.5 (c) shows the comparison of pass bandwidth of the existing and proposed triple band notched with single layer double U-slot scheme of interest. The existing antennas offer 2 notched bands, whereas the scheme of interest offered 3 bands in both the cases of when the substrate thickness is varied. The gain of the proposed and realized antenna configuration is higher than the existing antenna designs by 0.4 dBi with voltage standing wave ration of less than 2, similar to the existing scheme. The pass bandwidth of the triple band double U-slot antenna has been found to be 73%, whereas the existing antenna scheme has 83%. These results evidenced the superiority of the triple band notched double U slot antenna configuration.

4.5 SUMMARY

A small triple-band microstrip patch antenna has been proposed, designed and analyzed. The fundamental concepts of the microstrip patch antenna have been studied and the antenna has been realized. The proposed antenna configuration has been simulated using Ansoft HFSS version 13.0 software and the results have been analyzed. The results imply that the antenna exhibits three resonant modes and depending on the thickness of the substrate the operating bands are desired. The simulation results of the antenna scheme taken up for study refer several advantages of the scheme viz. smaller size, excellent radiation characteristics and circular polarization. For 1.6 mm thickness of substrate, the antenna scheme provides operating bands as 1.6 gigahertz, 1.9 gigahertz and 3.8 gigahertz. When the thickness is reduced to 37.5 % i.e. 0.6 mm, the operating bands achieved are 1.8 gigahertz, 2.2 gigahertz and 4.8 gigahertz. VSWR has been another parameter considered for the performance analysis. The proposed scheme offered VSWR less than 2. The results also exhibit that the bandwidth of 1.6 mm thickness substrate is 400 MHz, whereas the 0.6 mm thickness substrate resulted in 600 MHz.

The comparative analysis has been made between the existing antenna scheme and the proposed triple band notched with double U-slot, The analysis reveal that the proposed scheme provides 3 operating bands, even when the thickness of the substrates have been varied. Also, the gain and pass bandwidth of the proposed scheme are superior to the existing scheme. The VSWR of the proposed antenna configuration is found to be similar and in line with the existing antenna systems.

From the results it is clear that the operating frequencies are widely separated. This makes the triple layer technique not to provide sufficient bandwidth. In order to overcome this issue, multifunctional microstrip patch antenna with U-slots designed on a single layer substrate has been suggested in the fourth coming chapter. The aforementioned simulation results make evident that the proposed mutlipatch antenna scheme realized on a single layer with triple-band can be utilized widely for wireless communication applications.

CHAPTER 5

MULTIFUNCTIONAL PATCH ANTENNA

5.1 INTRODUCTION

The demand for integration of components including antennas of the wireless system has been increased due to the rapid development and revolution of the wireless technologies. Multifunctional patch antenna structures are being such kind, that incorporates U-slots to get multiple and wide bandwidths. These types of antenna structures holds good for multiple wireless applications viz. Global Positioning System (GPS), Wireless Local Area Network (WLAN), Worldwide Inter-operability for Microwave Access (WiMAX), Bluetooth etc. in this Chapter, a compact single layer microstrip line fed microstrip patch antenna with U-slot has been proposed, designed and analyzed for its performance evaluation. The proposed antenna scheme has been simulated using Ansoft HFSS version13.0 and the simulation results have been presented. The experimental validation of the proposed scheme has been fabricated and validated through network analyzer.

5.2 BACKGROUND STUIDES OF MULTIFUNCTIONAL PATCH ANTENNA

In wireless communication systems, antenna is the major component of the system. Miniaturization of the antenna plays a vital role particularly in the integrated low-profile wireless communication systems. It leads to an optimal design to meet the demanded output. Also it makes these antennas to be suitable for the next generation antenna technologies. The elementary structure of the microstrip patch antenna with a single-layer patch linearly polarized with wideband has been suggested by Huyun and Lee (1995). Hoorfar (2014) stated that two resonant frequencies can be approached when the air-gap length increases.

Lee *et al.* (2001), enhanced the performance of this geometry, such that it could cover multiple wireless technologies. They included U-slot in the microstrip patch, to enhance the bandwidth. The method of enhancing the bandwidth by introducing a band notch was not the interest of them. Their experimental results validated that; U-slot can be comfortably incorporated to a design an antenna with dual and multi-ban characteristics.

The other studies made by Lee K F *et al.* (2010) and Singh V K *et al.* (2013), illustrated that the U-slot patch antenna can be intended for wideband applications, but and for multiband applications. Vedaprabhu and Vinoy (2010), demonstrated the complexity to integrate multiple bands for wireless technologies. These complexities arose when the U-slot patch microstrip antennas are proposed for Advanced Wireless Services (AWS), Global System for Mobile (GSM) and various other WiMax and WLAN Bands. The reasons annotated that these applications operate at several frequency ranges and so it is complex to integrate multi bands.

The problem of designing antennas with narrow bandwidth has been addressed by Rao and Kumar (2011). They studied that increasing patch size increases the bandwidth of the antennas, when the antenna are designed with slits or slots. They proposed that this problem can be eliminated by using a a multiple layer dielectric substrate. Their results inferred that, the substrates added improved the bandwidth. Malikarjuna *et al.* (2015), in their research work on multilayer structure of patch antennas, concluded that the addition of substrate layers offers an enhancement in the impedance of the bandwidth and over desired frequency range the antenna possesses the same characteristics.

Yang Lu*et al.* (2011) suggested the techniques viz. multilayer microstrip antennas using a substrate with low dielectric constant to improve the impedance band-width and multiple frequency band of operation. Bo Li,*et al.* (2012) studied the design of multilayer stacked patch antennas for broadband applications. Lee K F (2011) presented a customized U-slot for the design of patch antennas with dual and triple bands of frequencies. Naesr*et al.* (2015) utilized double U-slot patch antenna with triple layer for wireless applications. During their research work, they studied the resonant behavior. It is specified that resonant behavior forms the coupling between two resonating modes in the dielectric regions through the air gap.Many researchers addressed the design of low-profile multi-band antennas. Their works have indicated that there are some drawbacks to be addressed in these antennas. In spite of the good radiation pattern exhibited by them, their fabrication costs and complexity are high.

The aforementioned characteristics, advantages and disadvantages, lead to an interest to propose a compact single layer microstrip line fed multifunctional patch antenna. The antenna is supposed to be in a miniature size with good radiation performance. The proposed antenna is to get multiple bands and wide bandwidth. The proposed structure is aimed for multiple wireless applications viz. GPS, WLAN, WiMAX, Bluetooth, RFID and telemetry, video and mobile communication applications.

5.3 MULTI-FUNCTIONAL PATCH ANTENNA

The far-reaching growth in the field of wireless communicationshas occasioned huge mandate for multi-band antennas. The antenna plays a vibrant role in the efficient incorporation of more than one communication standard in a single communication system. During the last few decades, printed, planar antennas have become a striking aspirant mainly because of interesting physical features such as simple structure, compactness and low manufacturing cost. In this research work, multifunctional microstrip patch antenna with operating frequencies of 1.5GHz, 1.99 GHz, 2.23GHz, 3GHz, 3.5 GHz, 3.9GHz, and 4.5GHz has been studied and analyzed.

Modern wireless systems entail extremely combined RF front-ends with the capability of multi-functional operation. There have been several efforts in the literature for designing the patch antenna with multifunctional characteristics as discussed in Section 5.2. Microstrip antennas are smart assemblies in RF communication systems due to weight, cost and profile. The most detrimental aspect of the microstrip antennas is their inherent narrow bandwidth.

The most popular technique to obtain a larger bandwidth is either to place parasitic elements next to the radiating element or to stack them vertically. When the operating frequencies are widely separated, such techniques may not provide sufficient bandwidth. In some applications, such as in the GPS, only a few distinct frequency bands are needed as opposed to a continuous operating frequency range. The purpose of this project is to introduce a novel multi-band microstrip antenna. This device relies upon a single dielectric layer instead of widely used multi-layer structure.

5.4 DESIGN OF MULTIFUNCTIONAL PATCH ANTENNA

The proposed compact multifunctional patch antenna is designed and fabricated as detailed here. In order to realize multi-band, two U-shaped slots have been created in at the surface of the radiator. The size and position of line feed are adjusted to obtain the desired multi-band characteristics.

5.4.1 Block Diagram of Proposed Antenna

The block diagram of the proposed antenna scheme is shown in Figure 5.1. The specifications that are needed to design the antenna include relative permittivity of substrate(ε_r), Resonance frequency (f_r) and Height of the antenna substrate (h). With these specifications, the length and width of the antenna are estimated, which are taken as input parameters to simulate the design using Ansoft HFSS. The simulated results are than analyzed through network analyzer.

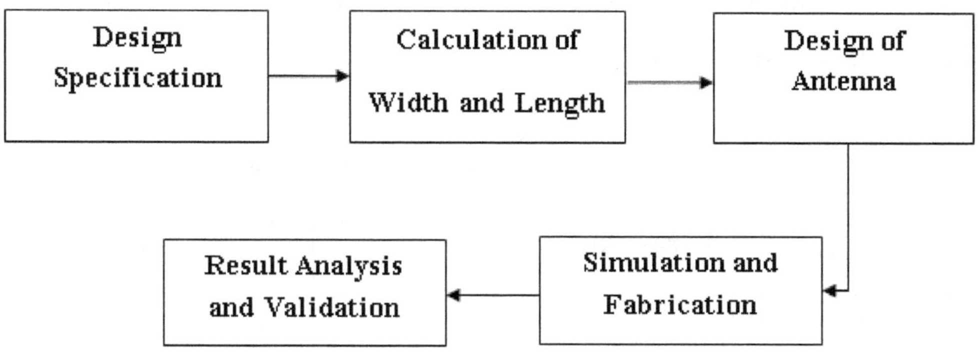

Figure 5.1 Block Diagram of Multifunctional Patch Antenna Design

5.4.2 Design Specifications

The microstrip patch antennas can be designed either by incorporating slots or introducing multiple layers. This design idea has been suggested by many researchers. The important parameters to be considered for the design of line feed rectangular patch antennas are, length (L_s) and width (W_s) of the substrate are estimated by selecting an appropriate resonant frequency (f_0), relative permittivity (ε_r) and height of the substrate (h_s). Form these parameters, the return loss and voltage standing wave ratios are calculated.

Many substrates with dielectric constants of the range 2.2 $\leq\varepsilon_r\leq$ 12 can be used for the design of microstrip antennas. Thick substrates with lower dielectric constants are preferred to provide good antenna performance. This is because, the thick substrate provides larger bandwidth, better efficiency and loosely bounded fields for radiation into space. In order to miniature the design, and for a microwave circuit, thin substrates are preferred. The thinner size substrates minimize the undesired radiation and coupling. Taking these factors into account, the required dielectric constant for the FR4 substrate is chosen as given in the Table 5.1. The other design parameters viz. resonant frequency and height of the substrate and the estimated length and width of the substrate are tabulated in Table 5.1.

Table 5.1 Design Specifications

Parameter	Value
Relative Permittivity	4.4
Resonant Frequency	1.8 GHz
Height of the substrate	1.59 mm
Width of the substrate	75.99 mm
Length of the substrate	65.17 mm

5.4.3 Design Implementation

The design and analysis of the proposed antenna is implemented through the estimated parameters estimated viz. length and width for the selected frequency, relative permittivity and height of the substrate. A rectangular patch of 48.5 × 37.2 mm^2 is etched on one side of a 1.6-mm-thick FR4 printed circuit board (PCB) substrate material, which has dielectric constant 4.4 and loss tangent 0.02 is displayed in Figure 5.2. The patch of the antenna is coupled strongly with the conducting ground plane, which enables the designed antenna to be capable of supporting multiple resonances. This antenna has a compact geometric profile of 76.6 × 65.2 mm^2. The design parameters required to study performance of the proposed multifunctional patch antenna using Ansoft HFSS version 13.0 have been tabulated in Table 5.2.

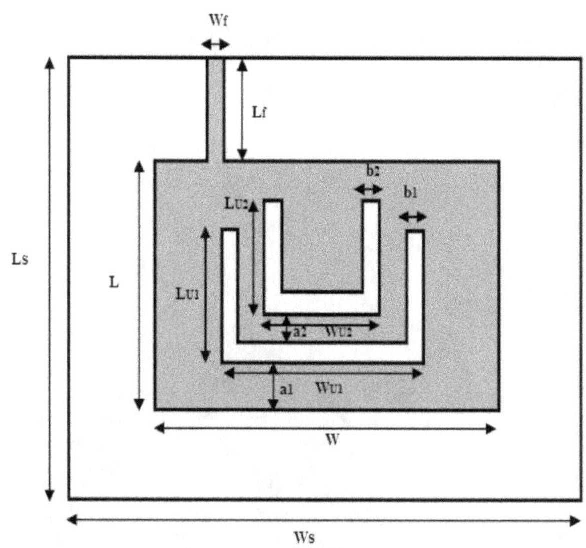

Figure 5.2 Geometry of Proposed Multifunctional Antenna Scheme

Table 5.2 Design Parameters

PARAMETERS	**SIZE (mm)**	**PARAMETERS**	**SIZE (mm)**
L_S	65.200	W_{U2}	12.000
W_S	76.600	a_1	4.600
L	37.200	a_2	4.000
W	48.6	b_1	2.000
L_{U1}	24.000	b_2	3.000
W_{U1}	20.000	L_f	14.000
L_{U2}	22.000	W_f	3.000

5.5 SIMULATION RESULTS AND DISCUSSIONS

5.5.1 Simulation Results

The proposed antenna scheme has been optimized for the design and simulated through Ansoft HFSS and the results have been analyzed. This design includes ground plane and U-slots on the surface of the radiator. The antenna is excited by the use of strip line feed. The simulated results have been portrayed in Figure 5.3.

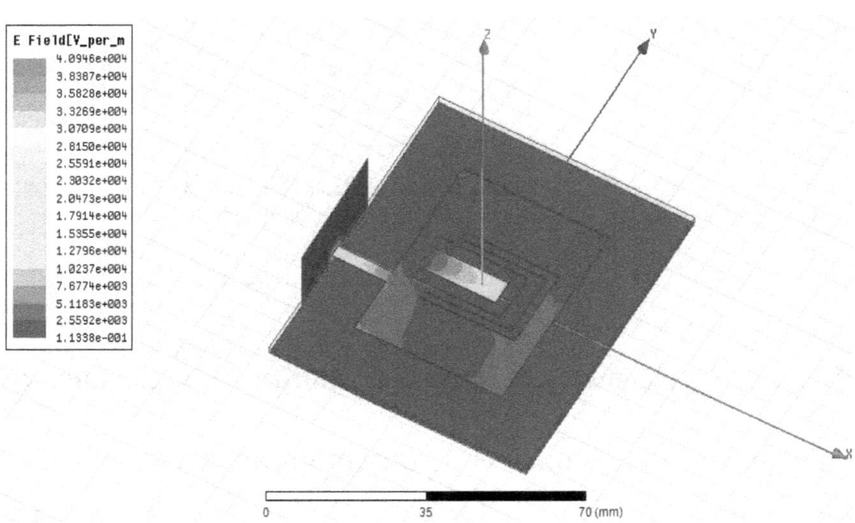

(a) Surface current distribution

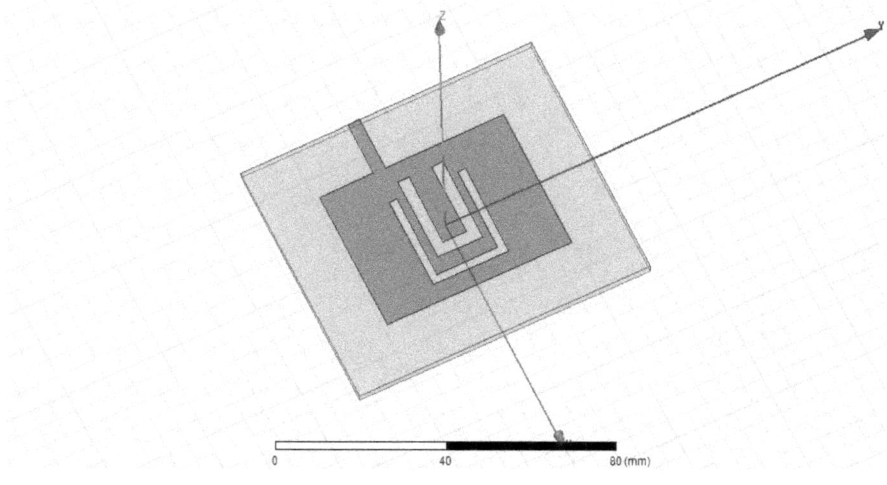

(b) Structure of Microstrip Line Feed

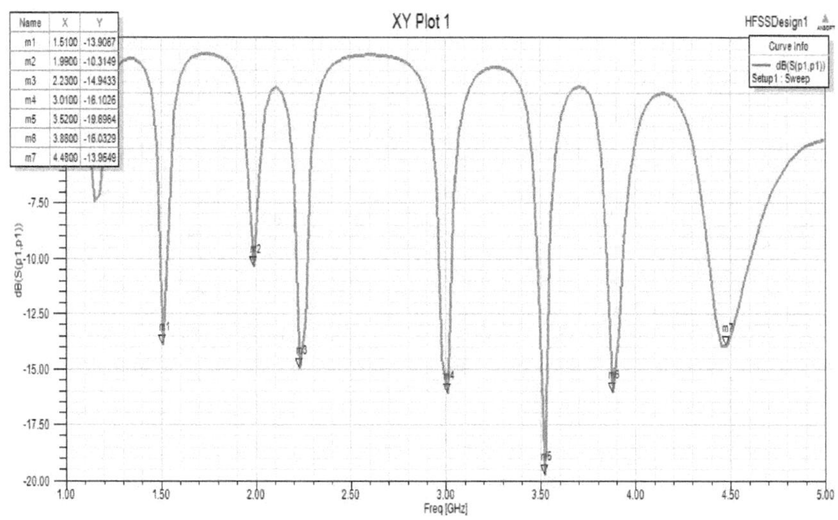

(c) Return Loss Curve

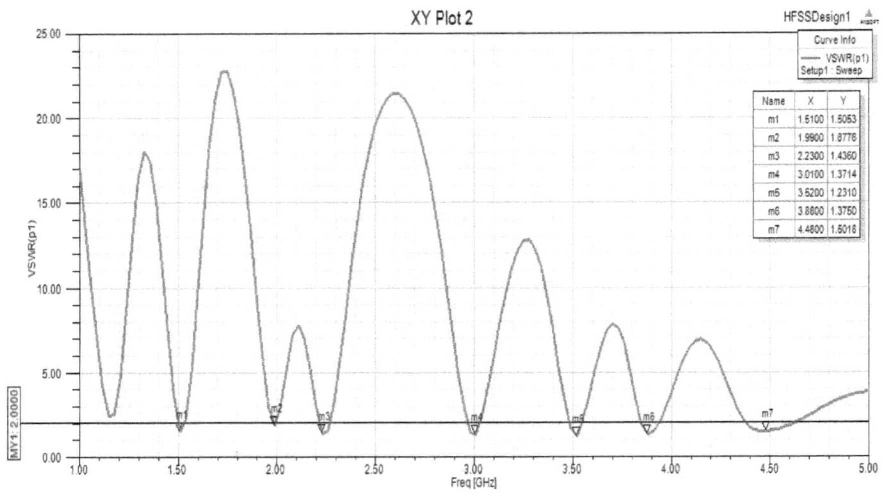

(d) VSWR Plot

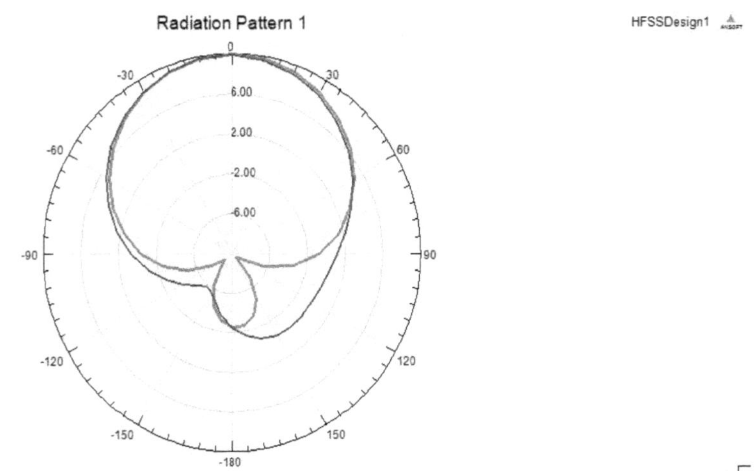

(e) Radiation Pattern in E-Plane

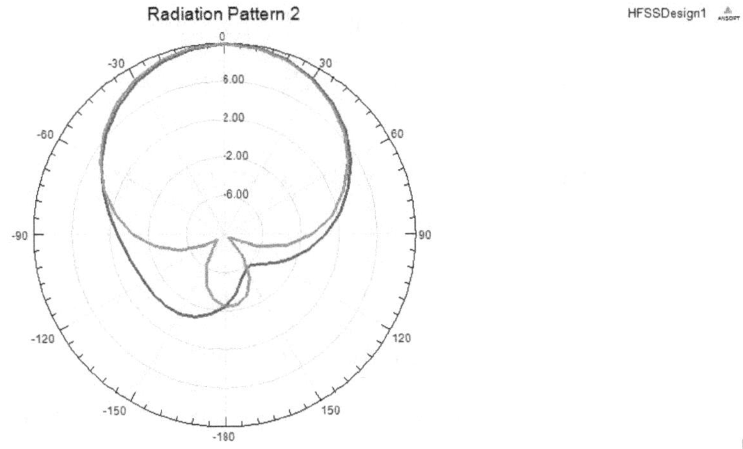

(f) Radiation Pattern in H-Plane

Figure 5.3 Simulation Results

5.5.2 Discussions

The surface current distribution, structure of microstrip line feed, return loss curve and VSWR plot simulated from the proposed design have been displayed in Figure 5.3 (a), 5.3(b), 5.3(c) and 5.3(d) respectively. From these results, it has been observed that the surface currents in the antenna are concentrated strongly around the double U-slots. This makes the antenna to effectively radiate current at 1.88 GHz operating frequency that achieves 4.096×10^4 V/m.

The simulated value of VSWR curve for the multi-band multifunctional patch antenna with two U-slots has been measured as less than 2 at consequent resonant frequencies. The return loss measurement and VSWR characteristics plots portrayed from the simulation results illustrates that the proposed antenna scheme achieves, achieves < -10 dB at all consequent frequency bands. Thus the proposed patch antenna can work in desired frequencies effectively. The radiation pattern resulted from the simulation model has been portrayed in Figures 5.3 (e) and 5.3 (f). It illustrates that the antenna can produce 8 dB gain at operating frequency of 1.88 GHz and produce directional radiation pattern at E and H planes.

5.6 HARDWARE IMPLEMENTATION

The simulated results have been experimentally validated, through a prototype model portrayed as in Figure 5.4. The hardware model has been fabricated with copper as the conductive layer and FR4 as the substrate as with thickness 1.6 mm. to achieve the characteristic impedance of 50Ω, the width and length of the patch is selected as 48.6 mm and 37.2 mm. The length and width of the feed line are chosen ad 14 mm and 3mm.

Figure 5.4 Prototype of Multifuncitonal Patch Antenna Scheme

5.6.1 Experimental Results

The fabricated antenna has been analyzed for its performance and the parameters were measured by N9926A Field Fox Handheld Vector Network Analyzer. The measured return loss, reflection coefficientand VSWR of the proposed multi-band patch antenna have been displayed in Figures 5.5 (a), 5.5(b) and 5.5 (c) respectively.

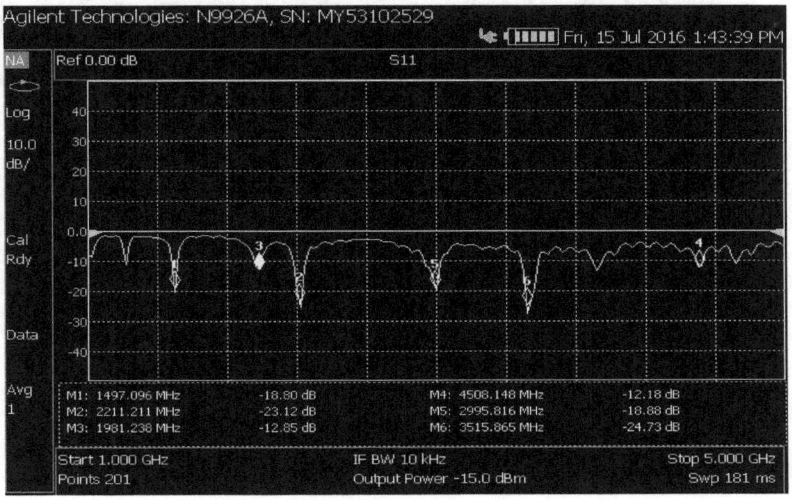

(a) Return Loss

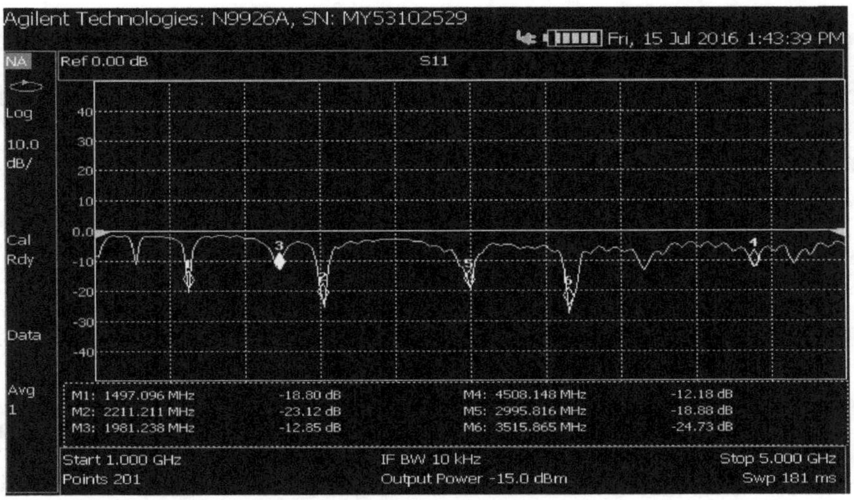

(b) Reflection Coefficient

(c) VSWR

Figure 5.5 Experimental Results

5.6.2 Discussions

From the measured results of the experimental prototype, it is evident that the proposed scheme achieves less than -10 dBat all desired operating frequencies. The measured VSWR resulted such that it achieves less than 2 at frequencies of 1.5GHz, 1.99 GHz, 2.23GHz, 3GHz, 3.5 GHz, 3.9GHz, and 4.5GHz.

5.7 COMPARATIVE ANALYSIS

A comparative study has been made between the simulated and experimentally measured values of the proposed multi-patch multifunctional patch antenna scheme. The comparative results have been portrayed in Figure 5.6. The simulated and experimental results show that the designed antenna has achieved a wide bandwidth with a return loss≤-10 dB for a frequency ranging from 1 to 5 GHz and VSWR<2. It demonstrates that the prototyped antenna will work effectively in the desired wireless applications. Thus the antenna is suitable for GPS, GSM, Bluetooth, WLAN, WiMAX, RFID and telemetry, video and mobile communications applications.

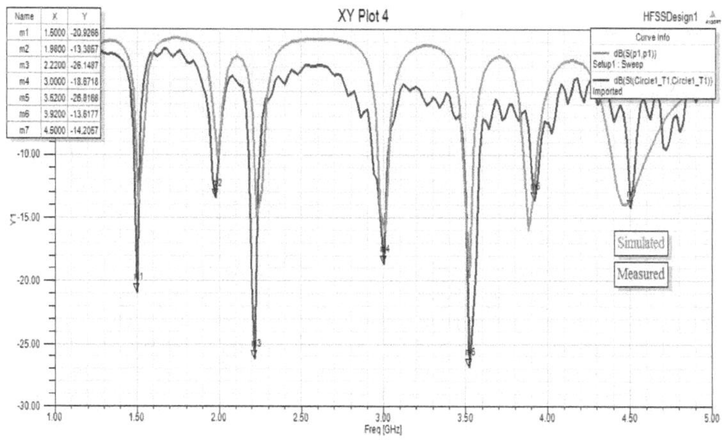

Figure 5.6 Comparative Analysis of Simulated and Experimental Results

Table 5.3 Comparative Analysis

Parameter	**Existing Antenna**	**Triple Band with Double U-Slot**	**Proposed multifunctional multiple Antenna**
Notched bands	2	3	7
Gain dBi	4.4	4.8	5.3
VSWR	< 2	< 2	< 2
Pass bandwidth	83%	73%	45%

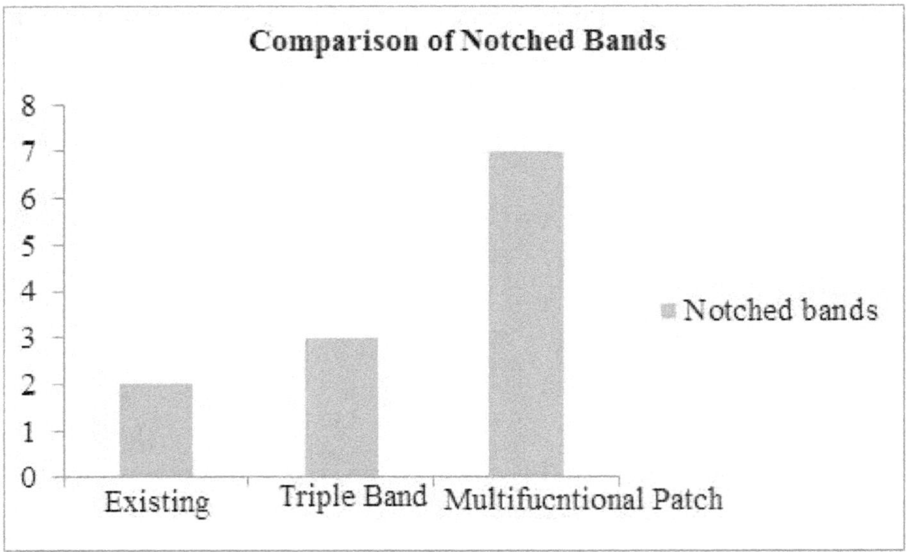

(a) Notched Bands

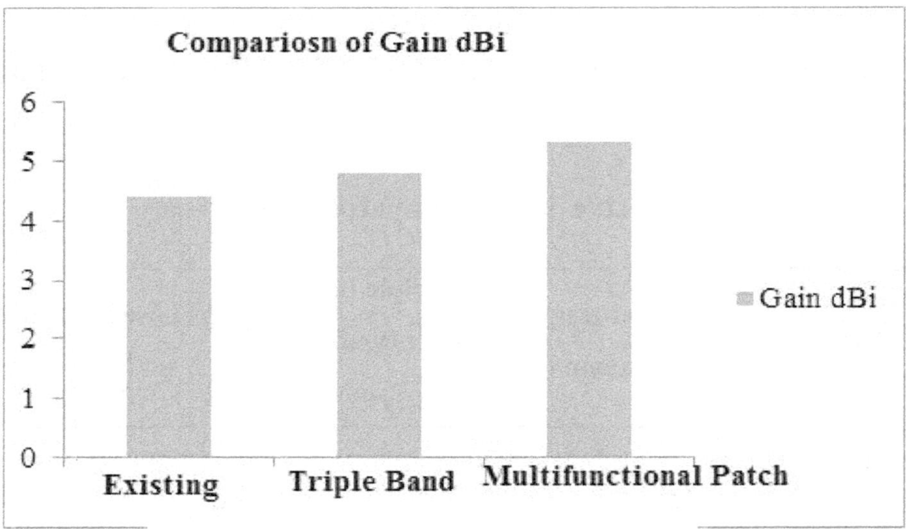

(b) Gain

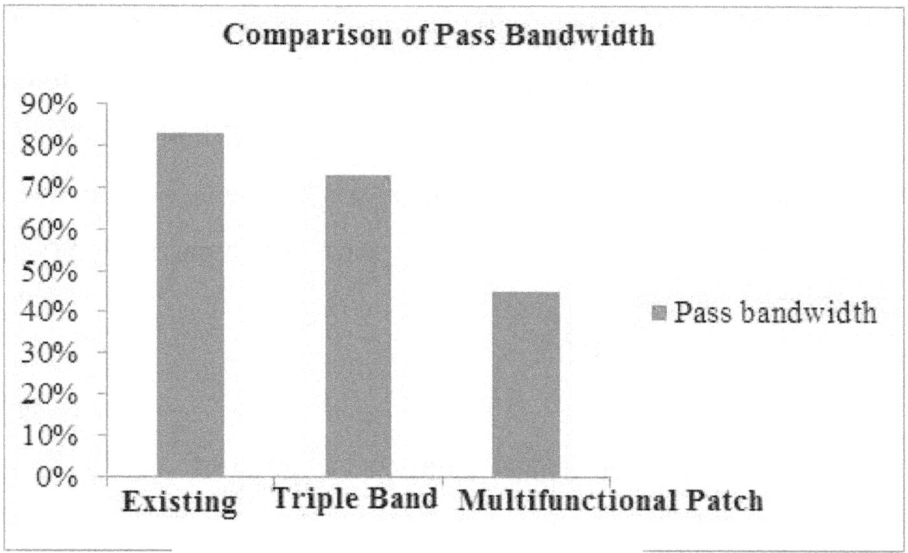

(c) Pass Bandwidth

Figure 5.7 Comparative Analysis

In this research work, the existing antenna scheme performance characteristics have been compared with the proposed antenna configurations of interest. The comparative analysis has been made among the existing antenna, triple-band double U-slot antenna and multifunctional double U-sot configurations. The results of the performance parameters have been tabulated in Table 5.3, for the configurations compared. Their corresponding analyses have been portrayed in Figure 5.7. The notched bands, gain and pass bandwidths have been displayed in Figure 5.7 (a), 5.7 (b) and 5.7 (c) respectively.

The existing antenna configuration provides only 2 bands of operating frequencies, while the triple band configuration provides 3. The multifunctional patch antenna with double U-slot offers 7 operating bands, which is higher than the three schemes compared. Similarly, the gain of the multifunctional patch double U-slot is higher as 5.3 dBi, whereas the existing and triple band offers 4.4 dBi and 4.8 dBi respectively. All the three configurations taken up for study have resulted VSWR as less than 2. Finally, the pass bandwidths of the configurations are 83% for the existing scheme, 73% for the tripe band configuration and its only 45% offered by the multifunctional patch double U-slot configuration. These results make them evident that the proposed multifunctional patch antenna with double U-slot in a single layer can be used effectively for wireless communication systems.

5.8 CONCLUSION

A compact planar multiband microstrip patch antenna using double U- slots has been proposed and investigated. The patch antenna with two U- slots has been designed and simulated using Ansoft HFSS Version 13.0. It has been fabricated on 1.6 mm thickness FR4 substrate. In this design, simple feeding such as microstrip line feeding technique has been used. The dimensions of U- slot and the feed position have been varied to provide impedance matching and to support multiple bands. The bands that are obtained for the center frequencies include 1.5GHz, 1.99 GHz, 2.23GHz, 3GHz, 3.5 GHz, 3.9GHz, and 4.5GHz. The simulated return loss and the VSWR for each of the center frequencies have been plotted. The radiation patterns in both the E-Plane and H-Planes have been analyzed. The experimental prototype model has been analyzed through network analyzer. The measured parameters have been compared with the simulated results. The simulated and measured results are in good agreement. These characteristics make the proposed single layer compact multifunctional mutlipatch antenna scheme as a good choice for portable communication devices.

Furthermore, comparative analyses have benne made among the existing, triple layer notched and multifunctional patch antenna with double U-slot antenna configurations. The comparative studies imply that the proposed multifunctional mutlipatch antenna scheme provides better performance indices as 7 operating bands, 5.3 dBi gain, VSWR less than 2 and 45% pass bandwidth. These parameters are superior when compared to the other schemes of interest taken up for study. These inferences conclude that the proposed single layer compact multifunctional multipatch antenna with double U-slot can be effectively used for GSM, WiMAX and WLAN communication systems

CHAPTER 6

COMPACT CPW FED TRIPLE-BAND ANTENNA

6.1 INTROUDCTION

Wireless communication devices are becoming more popular nowadays. They are widely used for voice and data communication. Based on the type of network, they are classified as GSM, Wi-Fi and WiMAX applications. Antennas become the fundamental component for the data transmission in these applications. The efficiency of the antenna plays a vital role in data transfer. In this Chapter, a compact co-planar waveguide(CPW) fed triple-band antenna has been proposed for the aforementioned applications. The design of the proposed system has been presented. The simulation model of the proposed antenna scheme has been evaluated through Advanced Design System (ADS) 10 software and the simulation results have been presented. The parameter taken up for study is the reflection coefficient, which is a measure of reflection by an electromagnetic wave due to impedance mismatch of the network. It is referred as S11 and measured in dB. The prototype model of the antenna structure of interest has been experimentally tested and the results have been compared with the simulation results.

6.2 CPW-FED ANTENNAS

In present scenario, without mobile phone nothing happens in the world. The mobile phone founds to be used in various applications viz. GSM, GPS, Wi-Fi, FM Radio, Bluetooth, WLAN applications, etc. for every application; a separate antenna cannot be designed. If so, it increases the size of the device. This creates a greater demand for an antenna with multiband operation. Such antennas become viral for combining multiple communication standards in a single compact wireless scheme. The antennas of these kinds simulate efficiently the compactness of the current personal communication systems. These factors attracted many researchers to focus on the design of ultra-wide bandantennas. Researchers began their work focusing on dual band rectangular monopole antenna for GSM and Wi-Fi applications. This antenna structures was later modified as CPW-fed Sierpinski gasket monopole antenna, which has a crooked U-designed strip and S-designed strip committed to the feed line. The three straight strips are implemented on the lowest layer with a rectangular ring. This forms the triple band antenna which is capable of operating at various frequencies such as 1.8 GHZ for GSM, 3.5 to 5 GHz for WiMAX and 2.45 to 5 GHz for WLAN applications.

The CPW fed antenna provides numerous exciting options like wider information measure, higher resistivity matching and simplest structure. The bimetal layer structure provides less bonding purpose and simply integrates with active devices of microwave monolithic integrated circuits. The CPW-fed structure thus provides a compact size for the antenna. The CPW-fed line consists of a single layer metallic structure with rectangular ring like S shaped strip connected to the feed line. Figure 6.1 illustrates the basic CPW-fed antenna structure.

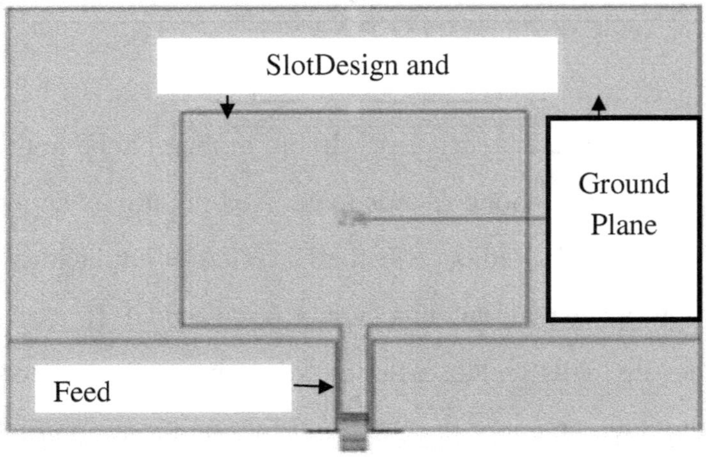

Figure 6.1 Basic Structure of CPW-Fed Antenna Scheme

6.3 REVIEW OF EXISTING CPW-FED ANTENNAS

Miniaturized dual-band coplanar waveguide (CPW)-fed antenna comprises of a rectangular patch that is enclosed by upper and lower ground plane sections that are connected by a high-impedance micro strip line. The antenna construction creates two distinct impedance bandwidths to cover frequency bands of GSM and Wi-Fi/WLAN. The antenna recognized is reasonably lesser in size (17x20 mm^2) and functions over frequency ranges 1.60–1.85 and 4.95–5.80 GHz, creating it appropriate for GSM and Wi-Fi/WLAN presentations. Furthermore, in the GSM band the antenna is circularly polarized. Investigational results of Naser-Moghadasi*et al.* (2013) revealedthat the proposed antenna scheme presents monopole-like radiation characteristics' and commendable antenna.

Xu Y *et al.* (2012) investigated an antenna structure with smaller reflection coefficient, of 210 dB Triple-band CPW-fed antenna for WiMAX and WLAN applications. This structure attained impedance bandwidths of 5.13–5.89, 3.07–3.82, and then2.34-2.50GHz. This scheme has a rectangular ring and an S-shaped strip committed to the feed line, through a crooked U-shaped strip and three straight strips on the bottom layer. The antenna has been efficiently fabricated and calculated. The investigated outcomes matches well with the simulated ones, precise good impedance matching and nearly omnidirectional radiation designs. Hong Chen *et al.* (2013) proposed a CPW-fed triband planar monopole antenna for WLAN/WiMAX applications. It comprises of monopole antenna printed on a substrate with two rectangular corners. The radiator of the antenna is precise compacted with an area of simply17x3.5 mm^2. Above that two L slots-inverted are imprinted to attain three radiating rudiments such that it will harvest three resonant modes for triband operation. By means of lesser size and modest structure, the actual and simulated outcomes indicate that this antenna has 10-dB impedance bandwidths of 120 MHz (2.39–2.51 GHz), 340 MHz (3.38–3.72 GHz), and 1450 MHz (4.79–6.24 GHz) to cover all the 2.4/5.2/5.8-GHz WLAN and the 3.5/5.5-GHz WiMAX bands. The results also attained the well-intentioned dipole-like radiation features exceeding the working bands.

Anil Kr Gautam*et al.* (2013) introduced a CPW-fed compact ultra-widebandmicro strip antenna for ultra wideband applications. This structure possesses a method to minimize the monopole antenna by stuffing of L-strip inverted above the traditional monopole patch antenna to lesser the antenna height. Towards two sides of the single radiator, the ground was perpendicularly stretched. Consequently, the huge space around the radiator that is generally unused can be efficiently protected. The antenna is virtually manufactured and simulated. Calculated outcomes display a good bargain with simulated outcomes. With whole size of 25x25x1.6mm^3 sample realizes worthy impedance toning, steady gain, stable radiation patterns, and constant group delay above a functioning bandwidth of 2.6-13.04 GHz.

The studies made by Pingan Liu*et al.* (2012), for WLAN plus WiMAX based compacted tri-band printed antenna comprises of an improved rectangular slot, a Y-shaped monopole radiator with a twisting split-ring slot and a couple of balanced inverted-L strips. Regulating the positions and the dimensions of these structures, three separate current paths can be created at three independent frequency bands, correspondingly. Focused on this observation, a model of the tri-band antenna is further made-up and calculated. The investigational and mathematical results reveal that the antenna has impedance bandwidth. That is on behalf of return loss less than 10 dB of 430 megahertz of the range 2.33 GHz to 2.76 GHz, 730 megahertz of the range 3.05 GHz to 3.88 GHz, and 310 megahertz of the range 5.57 GHz to 5.88 GHz. This cover both the WLAN 2.4/5.8-GHz bands and the WiMAX 2.5/3.5-GHz bands.

The above mentioned research studies ensure that the need for multiband antenna grows radically. In order to make a compact multiband antenna CPW feed is used in most of the research works. Among these, a small triple-band monopole antenna using a unique ground structure with the help of CPW feed will be targeted in this research work. An antenna by means of a rectangular ring in addition an S-fashioned strip committed to the feed line, through a crooked U-fashioned strip and three straight strips on the bottom layer was intended for triple band process. The antenna structure taken up for research study has been designed and analyzed using Advanced Design System (ADS) software.

6.4 ADS – AN OVERVIEW

Advanced Design System 12 (ADS) is leading electronic design automation software for Radio Frequency (RF) and power electronics applications. It can simulate the electromagnetic fields, currents and radiation patterns in an arbitrary 3D structure. The 3 structure comprises of metals, dielectrics, magnetic materials etc. This 3D Finite Element Method (FEM) allows it to be widely used in the industry for RF antenna and circuit designs. The industry standards of ADS are aimed at full-wave SPICE abstraction, in addition with S-parameter and for the high frequency electromagnetic simulation and for high-speed components. ADS' is broadly employed for the design of RF/microwave components, antennas, PCB interconnects, high-frequency IC packages, and on-chip embedded passives. ADS recover engineering production, decrease progress time, and improved guarantee in first-pass design. The modern publication of ADS conveys noteworthy production gains to Microwave/RF engineers and enlarges electromagnetic co-design to a new segment of engineers employed in the extents of RF/analog Integrated Circuit (IC) and multi-gigabit projects as well as Electromagnetic Interference (EMI) and Electromagnetic Compatibility (EMC).

6.4.1 Design Methodology

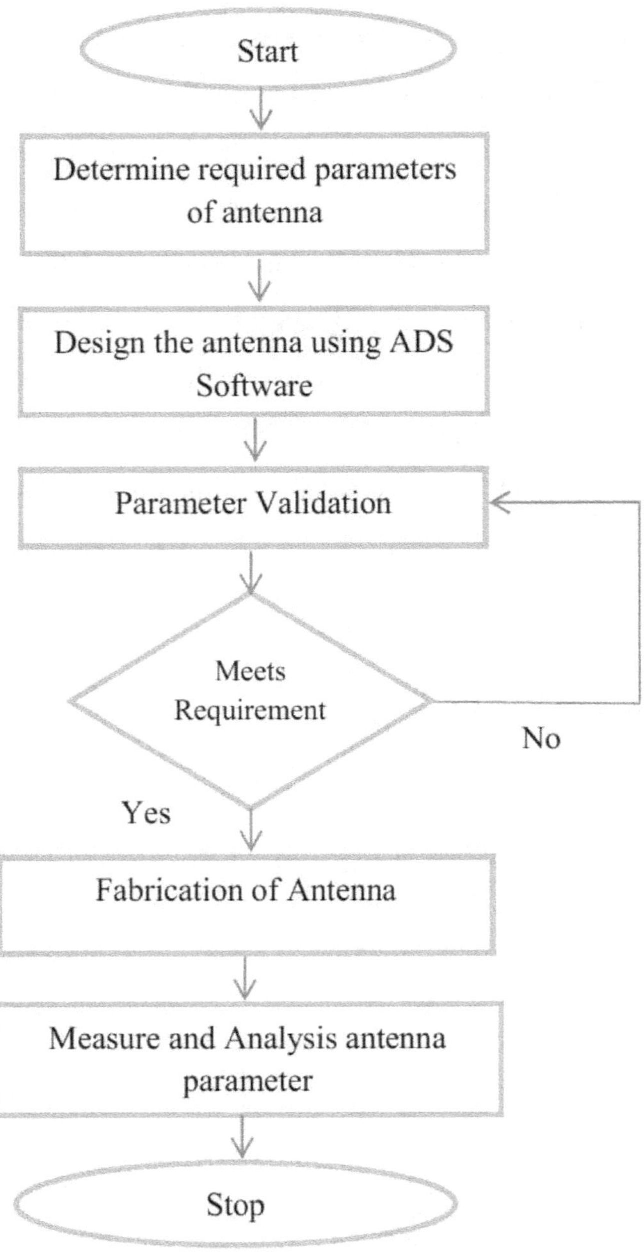

Figure 6.2 Flow chart of Design Methodology

The flowchart for the design of antenna through ADS is shown in Figure 6.2. In antenna design, the tenure of designed antenna of radiation pattern indicates the directional (angular) dependence of the (fields) strength of the radio frequency waves from the (transducer)antenna or extra sources. The design procedure is given as follows:

Step 1: Estimate the radiation efficiency W, for an effectual radiator with an applied width as per the Equation 6.1

$$W = \frac{1}{2f_r\sqrt{\mu_0\varepsilon_0}}\sqrt{\frac{2}{\varepsilon_r+1}} = \frac{v_0}{2f_r}\sqrt{\frac{2}{\varepsilon_r+1}} \qquad \text{Equ (6.1)}$$

Where,

v_0 = velocity of light of free-space in m/s

f_r = resonant frequency in Hz

ε_r = dielectric constant of the substrate

μ_0 = permeability of free space

ε_0 = permittivity of free space

Step2: Determine the effective dielectric constant of the microstrip antenna using Equation 6.2, based on the condition, $\frac{W}{h} > 1$

$$\varepsilon_{reff} = \frac{\varepsilon_r+1}{2} + \frac{\varepsilon_r-1}{2}\left[1+12\frac{h}{W}\right]^{\frac{1}{2}} \qquad \text{Equ (6.2)}$$

Step 3: Determine the additional or change in length required for W, by means of the Equation 6.3.

$$\frac{\Delta L}{h} = 0.412\frac{(\varepsilon_{reff}+0.33)\left(\frac{W}{h}+0.264\right)}{(\varepsilon_{reff}+0.258)\left(\frac{W}{h}+0.8\right)} \qquad \text{Equ (6.3)}$$

Step 4: Determine the length of the patch by resolving Equation (6.4)

$$L = \frac{1}{2f_r\sqrt{\varepsilon_{reff}}\sqrt{\mu_0\varepsilon_0}} \quad \text{Equ (6.4)}$$

Where, ε_{reff} is effective dielectric constant owing to fringing effect and ΔL is the extension in length due to fringing effect.

6.4.2 Proposed Antenna Strategy

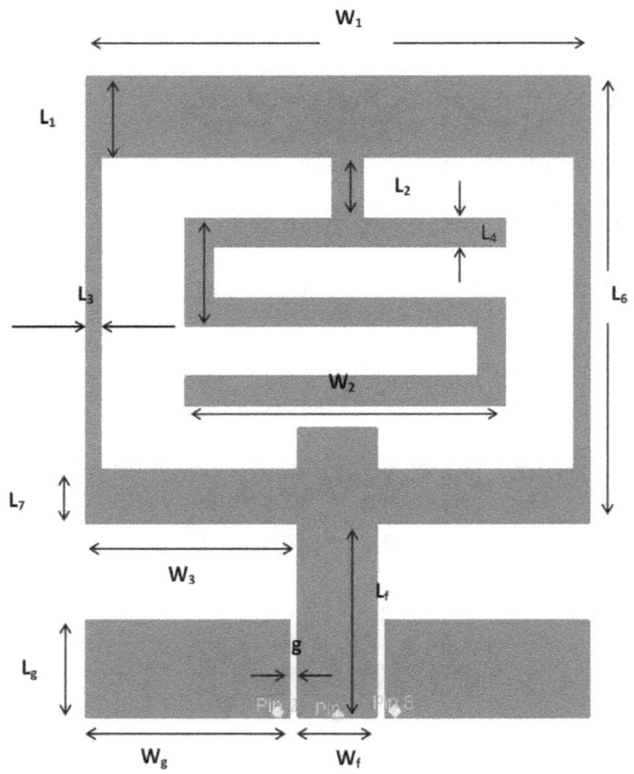

Figure 6.3 Geometry of Proposed Antenna Scheme

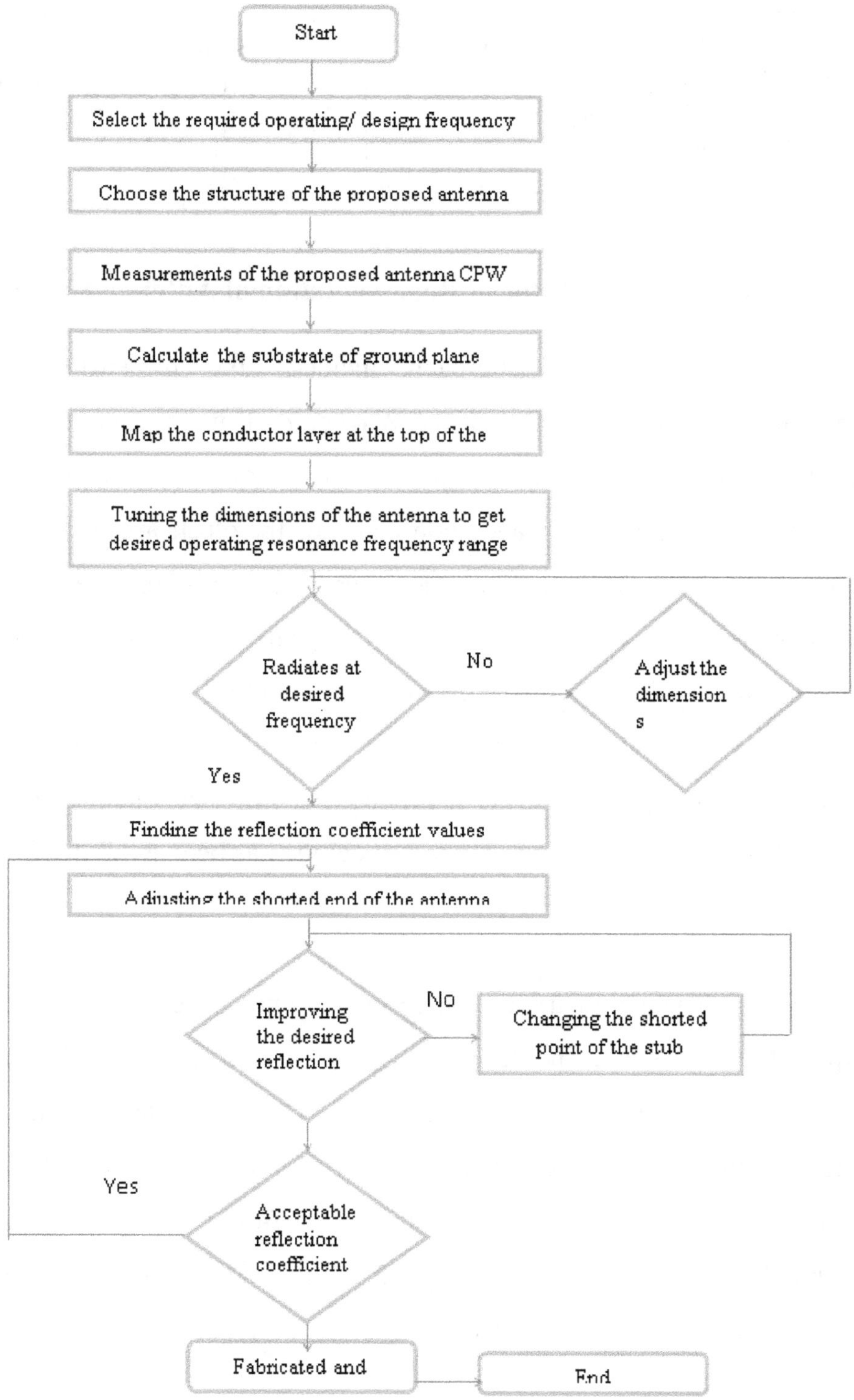

Figure 6.4 Proposed Antenna Design Flow

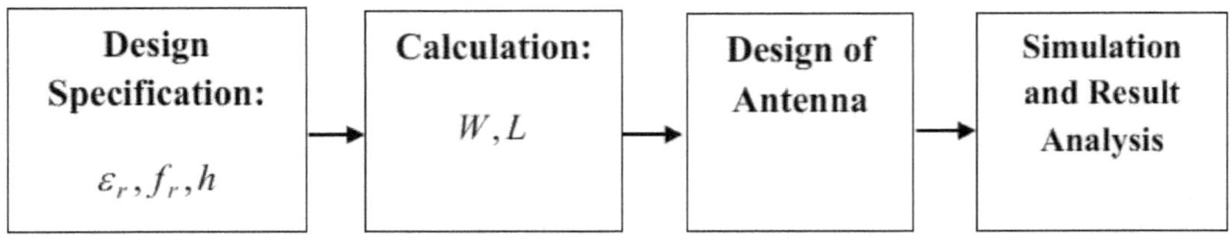

Figure 6.5 Pictorial Representation of Antenna Design

The design approach includes the dimensioning of the waveguide. The dimensioning of the Waveguide Printed reception apparatuses for the most part utilized with coplanar waveguides to exchange the received or transmitted signs. The waveguide manages the electromagnetic waves over a specific distance. It is an uncommon type of transmission line that exists in a few configurations and can be made utilizing the printed circuit innovation. A coplanar waveguide comprises of a focal conductive line encompassed by the ground plane on the two sides of the substrate. The waveguide must present characteristics impedance of 50 Ω to meet the proposed antenna. A model that allows finding the impedance of the waveguide has been exhibited by W C Liu (2005).

The geometry of the proposed antenna configuration has been exposed in Figure 6.3. The design comprises of a ring (rectangular) and a strip (S-shaped omitted to the CPW feed line. The parameters of the proposed antenna scheme have been tabulated in Table 6.1. Figure 6.4 illustrates the pictorial representation of the antenna design flow and Figure 6.5 represents the block diagram of antenna design. From the parameters tabulated in Table 6.1, the antenna design is carried out.

Table 6.1 Parameters of the proposed antenna

Parameters	Size (mm)
L_1	02.75
L_2	01.89
L_3	03.02
L_4	0.899
L_5	1.255
L_6	6.01
L_7	1.702
L_f	6.01
L_g	3.01
W_1	15.92
W_2	9.27
W_3	6.8
W_f	2.51
W_g	6.49
G	0.249
H	1.612

The simulation package used in this research work is Agilent's ADS. The design steps are similar to the other simulation packages. The technique followed is as given below:

Step 1: Stipulate

Substrate Dielectric (ε_r)

Antenna Resonant frequency (f_r)

Substrate Height (h)

Step 2: Regulate

Patch Width (W)

Patch Length (*L*)

Step 3: Start the Agilent's ADS (2011) software and create a new workspace.

Step 4: Set the measurement unit for the model as millimeter.

Step 5: Create the substrate medium with relative permittivity ε_r as 4.4 and set its thickness as 1.6mm.

Step 6: Map the conductor layer at the top of the substrate.

Step 7: Assign the upper and lower medium of the substrate as air.

Step 8: Construct the S-Shaped strip and Rectangular Ring as patch at the top of the substrate.

Step 9: Construct a pair of symmetrical Ground plane at the top of the substrate at both sides of the feed line of patch.

Step 10: Create three ports, one at signal plane, and other two are at either ground planes as P_1, P_2, P_3 respectively.

Step 11: Assign 50Ω impedance for P_1 and 0Ω for P_2 and P_3 ports.

Step 12: Set P_2 and P_3 as reference for the port P_1.

Step 13: Set the continuous frequency as 1.60-5.80 GHz.

Step 14: Union of all the elements are created.

Step 15: Simulate the design using EM simulator.

Step 16: Analyze the Results.

The antenna width is chosen ad 1.6 mm and is etched on the top of the substrate. The dielectric constant of the substrate is ε_r =4.4 and the FR4 component is used as substrate material. The dimension of the projected antenna is 16 x 20 mm^2. The design parameters are optimized using the Agilent's ADS software.

6.5 SIMULATION RESULTS AND DISCUSSIONS

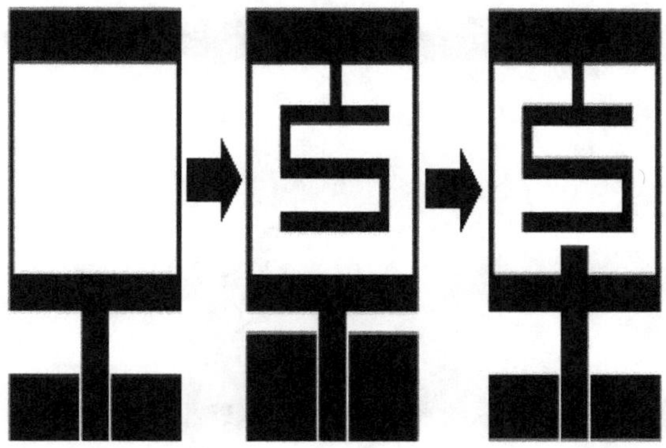

(a) Style Evolution of Planned Antenna

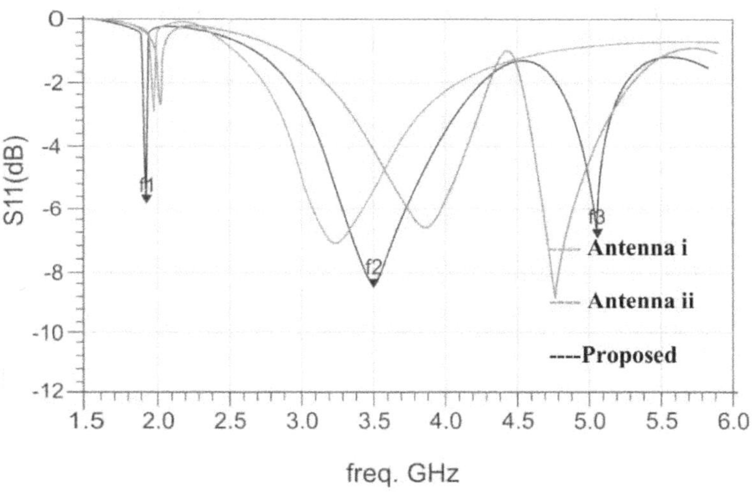

(b) Reflection Coefficient

(i) 1.85 GHz (ii) 3.5 GHz (iii) 5.1
GHz

(c) Field Distribution Pattern

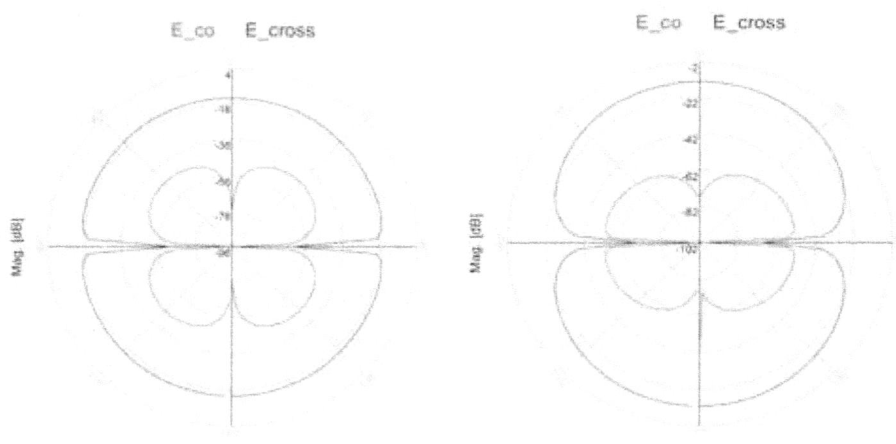

(i) XY Plane (ii) YZ Plane

(d) Radiation Pattern at 1.85 GHz

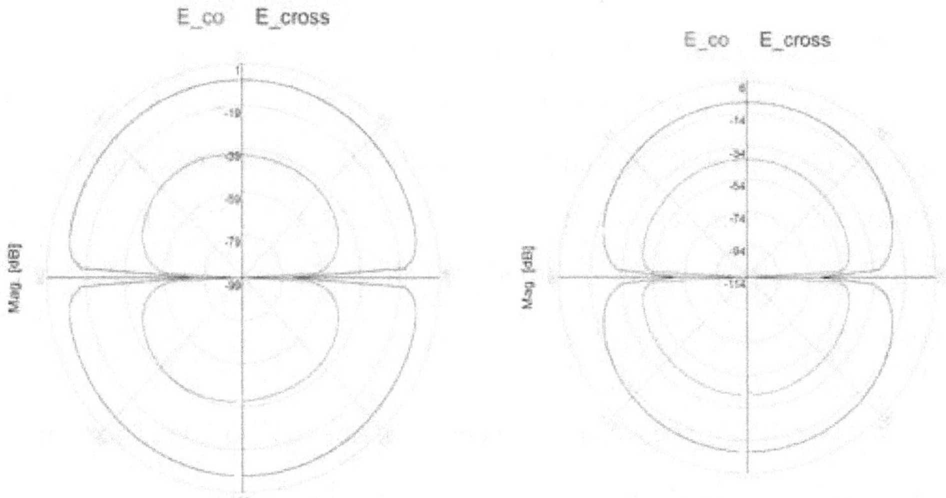

(i) XY Plane (ii) YZ Plane

(e) Radiation Pattern of 3.5 GHz

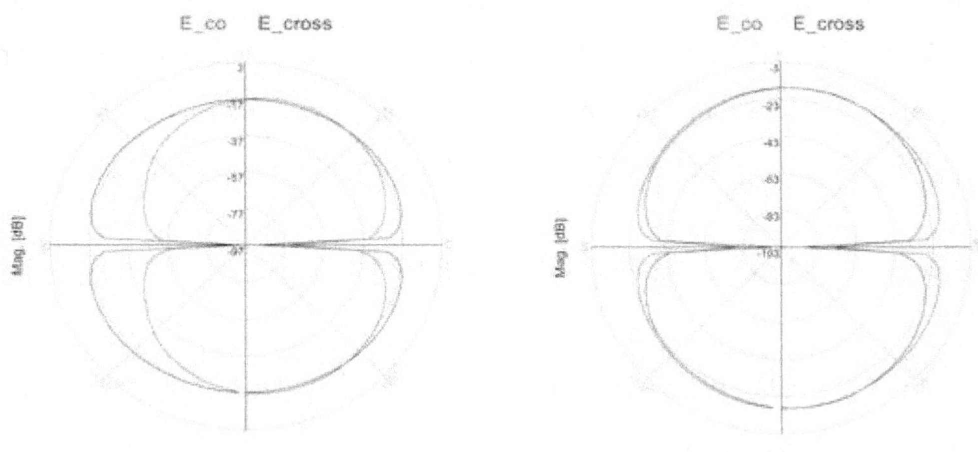

(i) XY Plane (ii) YZ Plane

(f) Radiation Pattern of 5.1 GHz

Figure 6.6 Simulation Results

The evolution of the planned antenna vogue and their simulated reflection co-efficient area unit are displayed in Figures 6.6 (a) and 6.6 (b) respectively. The results portrayed that the proposed antenna pattern (i) and

(ii) have exclusively rectangular ring and it's being operated over 3.441GHz to 3.60GHz band. Addition of the S-shaped strip in the antenna patterns makes the antenna to be operated at three resonant frequencies such as 1.85 GHz, 3.5 GHz and 5.1 GHz. The need for the study of two antenna patterns is to make the antenna scheme applicable for GSM, WiMAX and WiFi band applications. The parameters have been varied and the optimized parameters have been proposed in Table 6.1.

The performance indices of a linearly polarized antenna include the radiation patterns in E and H planes. The E plane tracks the extreme radiation pattern in the plane with electric field vector. The H lane points the way of maximum radiation in the plane of magnetic field vector. The field distribution of the proposed antenna scheme at the aforementioned resonant frequencies and the radiation patterns have been portrayed in Figures 6.6 (c), 6.6 (d), 6.6 (e) and 6.6 (f). The simulation results portrays that the proposed antenna scheme can be operated at resonant frequencies of 1.85 GHz for GSM, 3.50 GHz for WiMAX and 5.10 GHz for WiFi applications.

6.6 HARDWARE IMPLEMENTATION

The proposed antenna scheme has been fabricated with the optimized parameters as mentioned in Table 6.1. The portrait of the fabricated antenna triple band CPW fed antenna scheme has been portrayed in Figure 6.7. The fabricated CPW fed antenna shows that it can effectively operate at designed frequency ranges. The photograph illustrates that the proposed antenna scheme has relatively small dimensions and operates at desired frequency ranges.

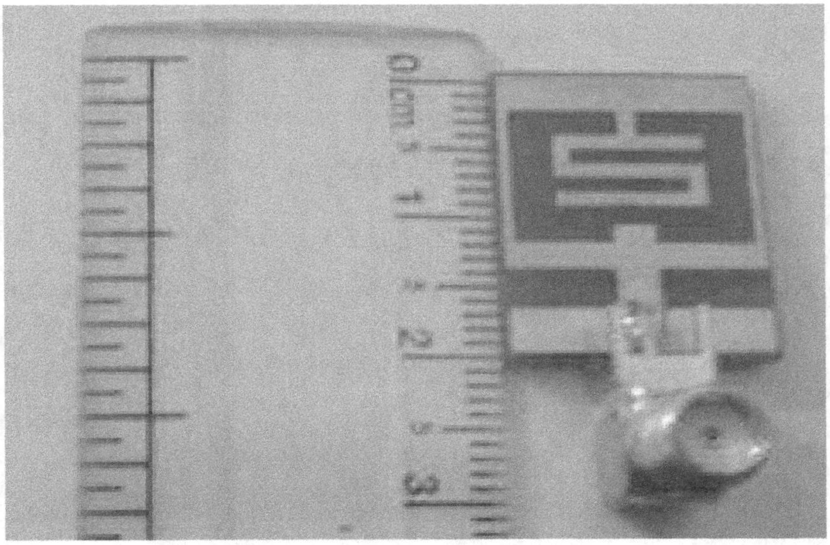

Figure 6.7 Portrait of Fabricated Triple Band CPW Fed Antenna

6.6.1 Results

The realized hardware system of the proposed antenna configuration has been tested and analyzed using Agilent's Network Analyzer. The perfromance indices vis. Retrun oss, voltage standing wave ratio and the smit chart analysis have been observed and protrayed as in Figure 6.8 (a), 6.8 (b) and 6.8 (c) respectively.

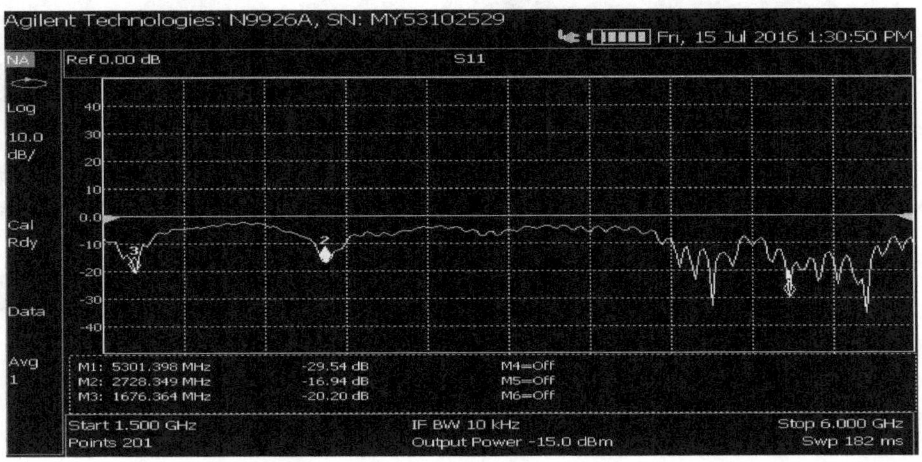

(a) Return Loss

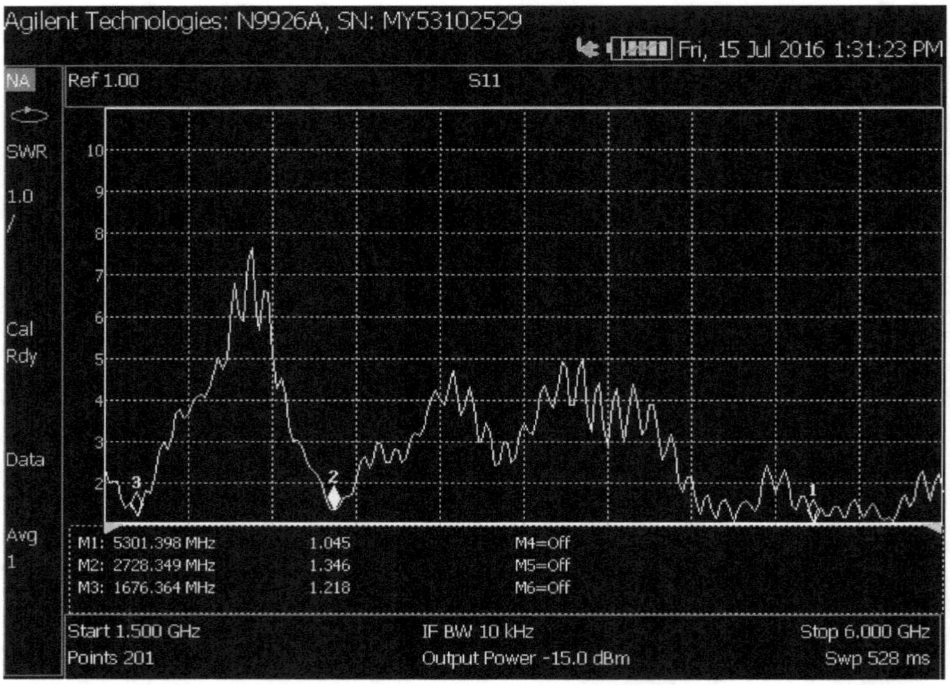

(b) Voltage Standing Wae Ratio

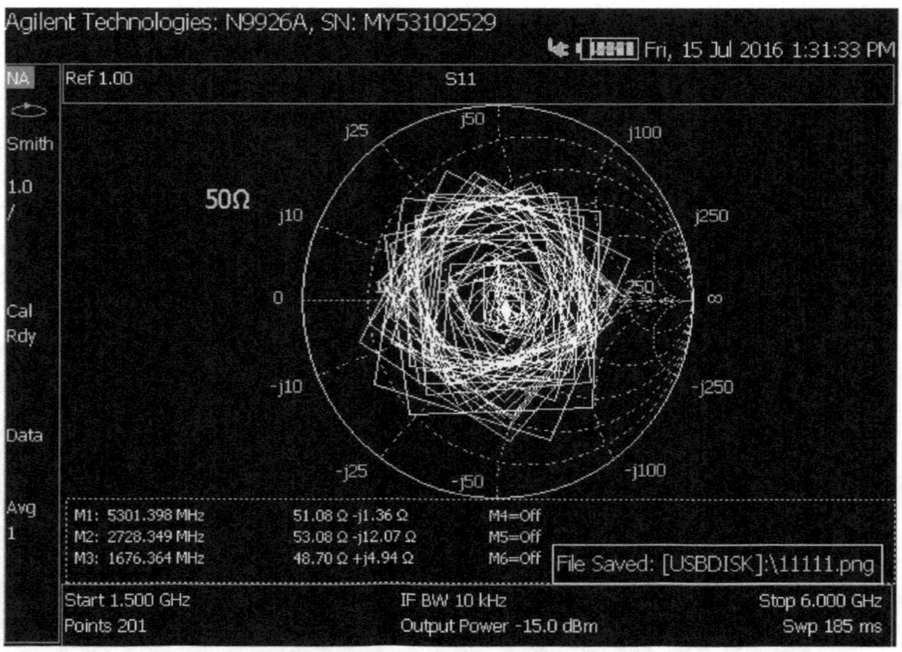

(c) Simth Chart Analysis

Figure 6.8 Results from Network Analayzer

6.7 ANALYSIS

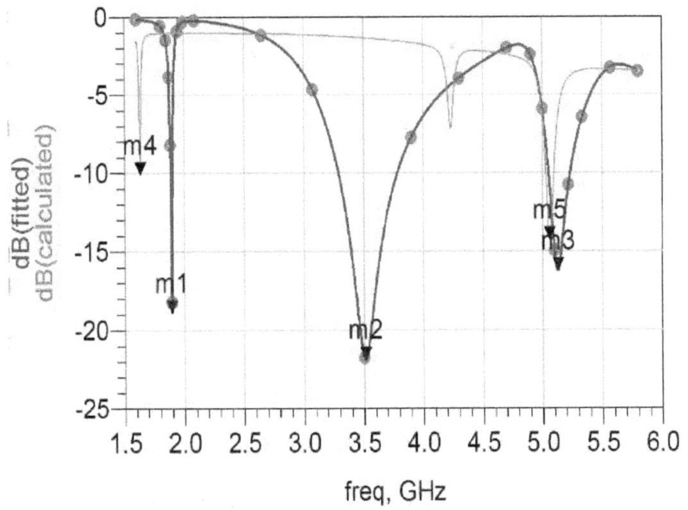

(i) Antenna 1

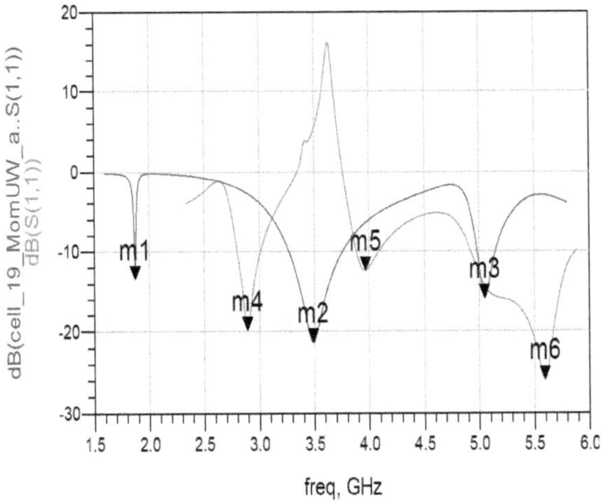

(ii) Antenna 2

(a) Reflection Coefficient of Antennas

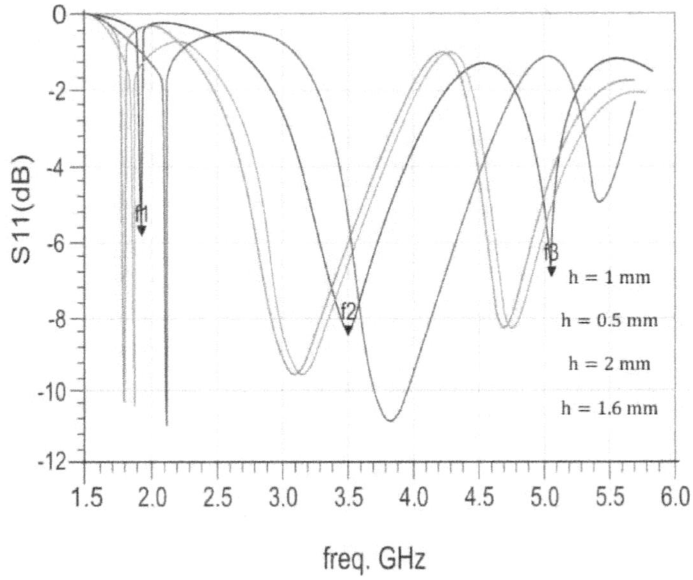

(i) Variation in Height of the Substrates

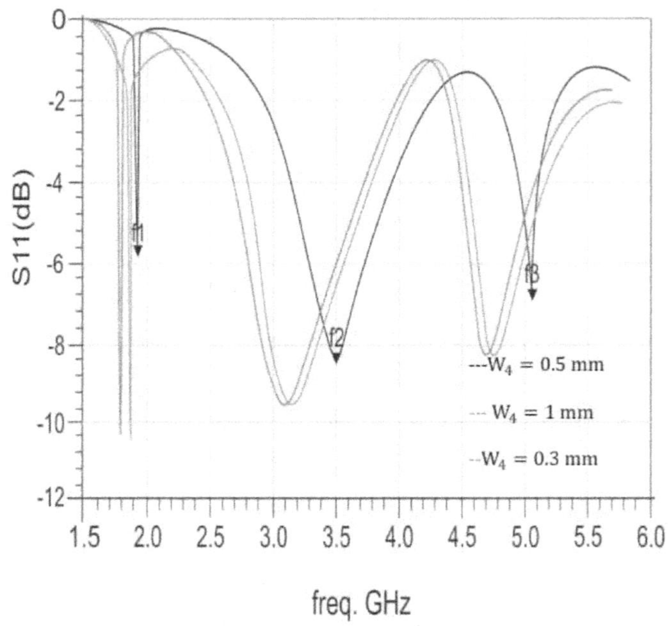

(ii) Variations in Width of the Substrate

(b) Reflection Coefficient variations with reference to height and width of the substrates

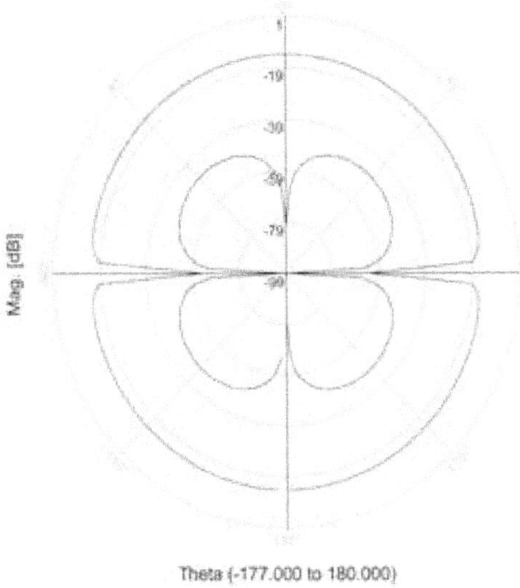

(i) XY Plane

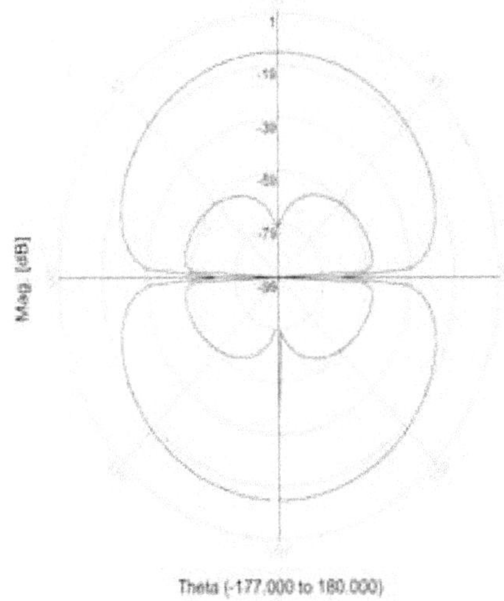

(ii) YZ Plane

(c) Radiation Patterns of fabricated antenna schemes at 1.85 GHz

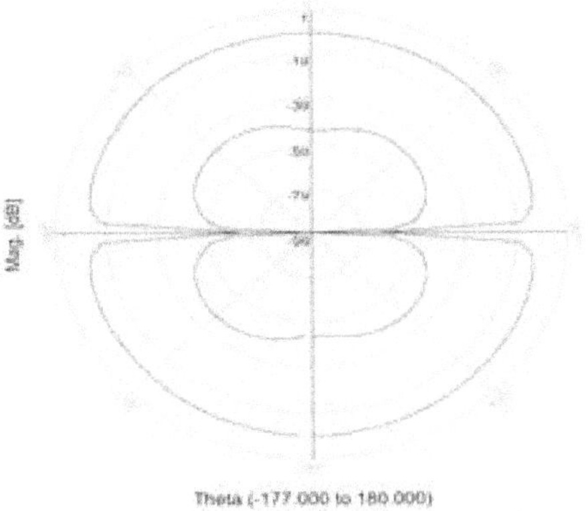

(i) XY Plane

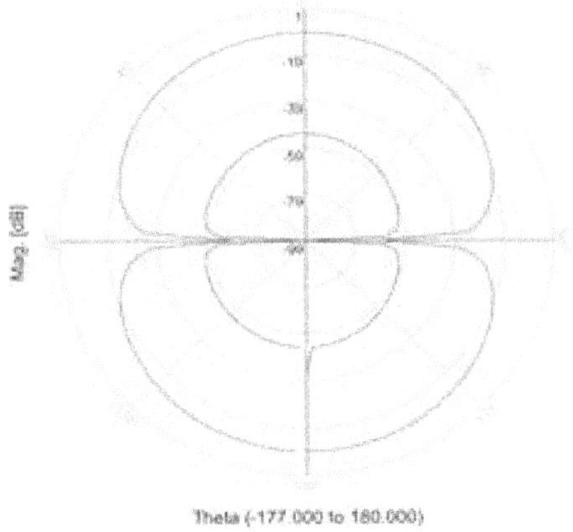

(ii) YZ Plane

(d) Radiation Patterns of fabricated antenna schemes at 3.5 GHz

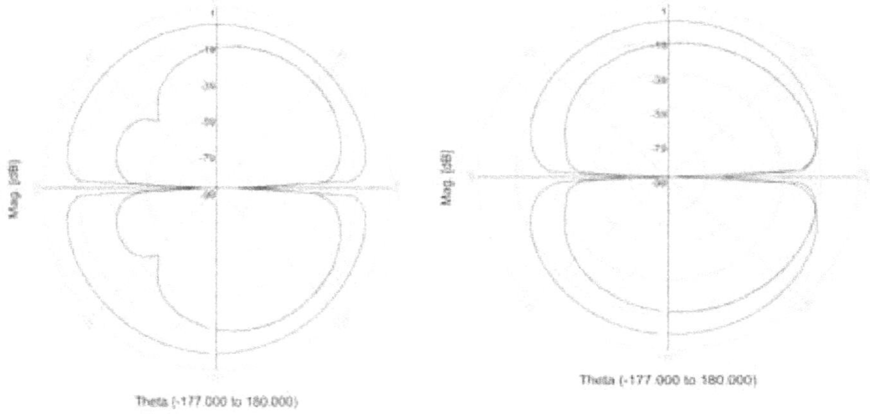

(i) XY Plane (ii) YZ Plane

(e) Radiation Patterns of fabricated antenna schemes at 5.1 GHz

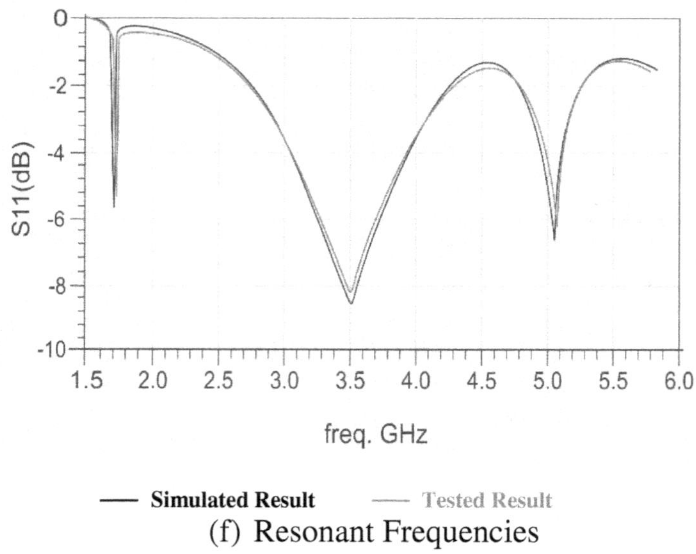

(f) Resonant Frequencies

Figure 6.9 Comparative Analyses of Simulated and Experimental Results

Figure 6.9 compares the results of fabricated hardware and simulated antenna schemes. Figure 6.9 (a) exhibits the reflection coefficient variations of the antenna 1 and antenna 2. Figure 6.9 (b) displays the variation of reflection coefficients with reference to the change in dimensions height and width of the substrates. Figure 6.9 (c), 6.9 (d) and 6.9 (e) reflects the comparison of radiation patterns at the resonant frequencies 1.85 GHz, 3.5 GHz and 5.1 GHz respectively. The achievement of the corner frequencies of the simulation and hardware prototype has been shown in Figure 6.9 (f). These results have been measured using the network analyzer.

The experimental results show that the operative frequencies square measure obtained at 1.85 GHz, 3.50GHz and 5.10 GHz, with reflection co-efficient of -10dB.For additional analysis, the simulated co-efficient difference for changes among the peak of the substrate as shown in Figure 6.9 (b) illustrates that the variation in dimensions affect the reflection co-efficient of the planned design. From the Figure 6.9 (b) the optimized price of h and W_4 unit of measurement has been found to be 0.51 millimeter individually. From these graphs, the proposed design gives good performance over others with compact size. The results conclude that the proposed triple band CPW fed antenna operates at multiband frequencies.

6.7.1 Comparative Analysis

Table 6.2 Comparative Analysis of existing and CPW-fed antenna scheme

Parameter	Existing Antenna	Proposed Antenna
Notched bands	2	3
Gain dBi	4.4	5.2
VSWR	<2	<2
Pass bandwidth %	60	81

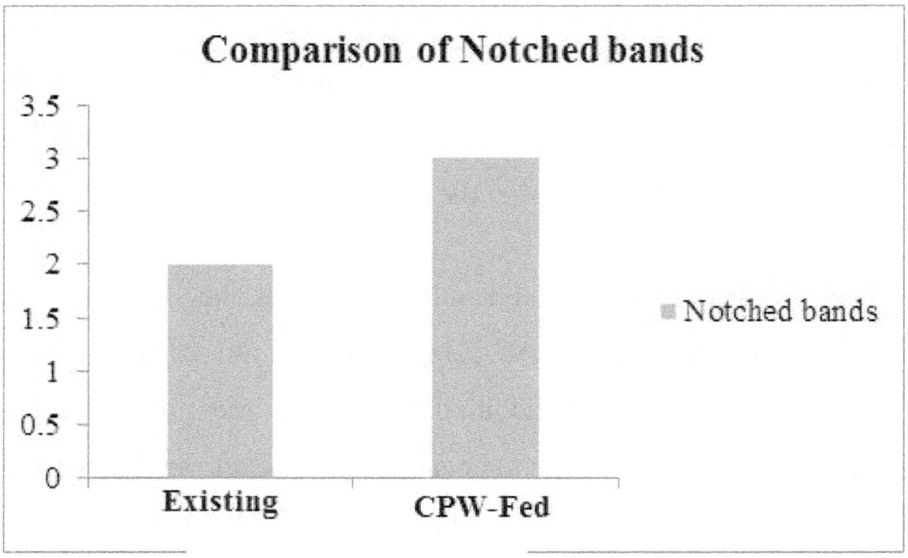

(a) Notched Bands

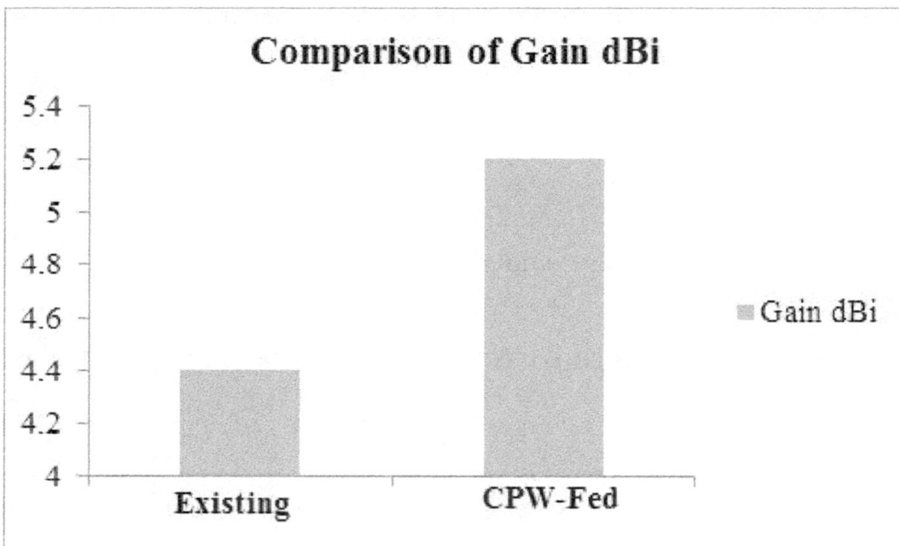

(b) Gain

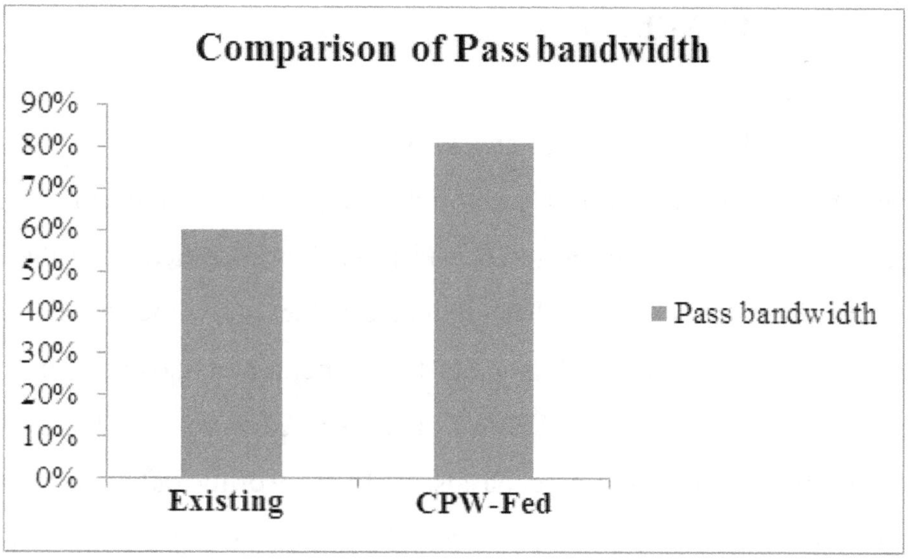

(c) Pass Bandwidth

Figure 6.10 Comparative Analyses of various antenna schemes

A comparative study has been made between the existing antenna scheme and the proposed compact triple band CPW-fed microstrip patch antenna scheme. The performance indices taken up for analysis have been tabulated in Table 6.2. Their corresponding analyses have been displayed in Figure 6.10. The operating bands have been displayed in Figure 6.10 (a). The comparison between the systems on the aspects of gain and pass bandwidth have been portrayed in Figures 6.10 (b) and 6.10 (c) respectively. The results portrays that the proposed triple band CPW fed antenna scheme has 3 notched bands with higher gain of 5.2 dBi. The existing system offers only 2 operating bands and with a lower gain of 4.4 dBi. The VSWR of both the systems are in line with each other as because both system exhibits VSWR of less than 2. The results also reveal that the pass bandwidth of the proposed triple layer CPW-fed antenna scheme is 81% which is slightly lesser than the existing scheme. The existing scheme offered 60%. These results portray the superiority of the proposed compact triple band CPW fed microstrip patch antenna.

6.8 CONCLUSION

For GSM, Wi-Fi and WiMAX applications, a compact CPW-fed triple-band antenna has been proposed. The pioneering antenna comprises of rectangular ring in addition to an S-fashioned strip dedicated to the feed line on the top of the substrate. The simulated values show that the demonstrated antenna can successfully obtained at three operating bands covering 1.8 GHz for GSM, 3.5 GHz for WiMAX and 5.1 GHz for Wi-Fi applications. Moreover, the projected antenna also delivers worthy radiation patterns and stable gains in the operative bands. This compact triple-band antenna is a suitable aspirant for wireless communication schemes. The projected antenna has many benefits like tiny size and magnificent radiation characteristics. The simulation results have been validated through experimental design and analysis.

The proposed antenna configurations have been analyzed through Agilent's network analyzer and the results have been displayed and analyzed. To demonstrate the superiority of the proposed compact triple-band CPW-fed antenna configuration, comparative analyses have been made with the existing scheme. The results have been tabulated and analyzed. The proposed CPW-fed antenna offered triple band with high gain of 5.2 dBi. These parameter indices are higher compared to its existing counterpart. The voltage standing wave ratios of both the configurations of interest exhibit VSWR less than 2 and are in line with each other. The pass bandwidth of the proposed CPW-fed antenna design is better as 81% which is 83% for the existing system design. The results exhibit the enhanced characteristics of the proposed antenna scheme, which makes the proposed antenna to be suitable for GSM, WiMAX, Wi-Fi and WLAN applications.

CHAPTER 7

PERFROMANCE ANALYSIS

7.1 INTRODUCTION

In this chapter, the performance analyses have been made among the conventional, proposed compact microstrip line-fed ultra-wide band antenna scheme with triple notched band, compact single layer triple band and microstrip line fed multifunctional patch antenna with U-slots and compact CPW – fed triple-band antenna. The first three schemes of interest showed the number of bands notched and whereas, the compact CPW-fed triple band antenna scheme studied the passbands.

7.2 COMPARATIVE ANALYSIS

Two comparative analysis have been made in this research work,

a) Among the existing and the three proposed schemes, as they aimed to study the band notched system.

b) Between the existing and proposed CPW-fed antenna scheme, as this scheme aimed to study the pass band frequencies.

7.2.1 Band Notched Antenna Systems

Table 7.1 portrays the measured values of the fabricated antenna arrangements taken up for study under band notch classification. The proposed antenna configurations have been compared with the existing system in order to validate the effectiveness of the proposed schemes. The performance indices considered for the validation include number of notched bands, gain in dBi, VSWR and pass bandwidth.

Table 7.1 Comparative Analysis of Band Notched Systems

Parameter	**Existing Antenna**	**Microstrip triple ultra-wide band Antenna**	**Triple Band with Double U-Slot**	**Multifunctional multiple patch Antenna**
Notched	2	3	3	7
Gain dBi	4.4	5.2	4.8	5.3
VSWR	< 2	< 2	< 2	< 2
Pass bandwidth	83%	62%	73%	45%

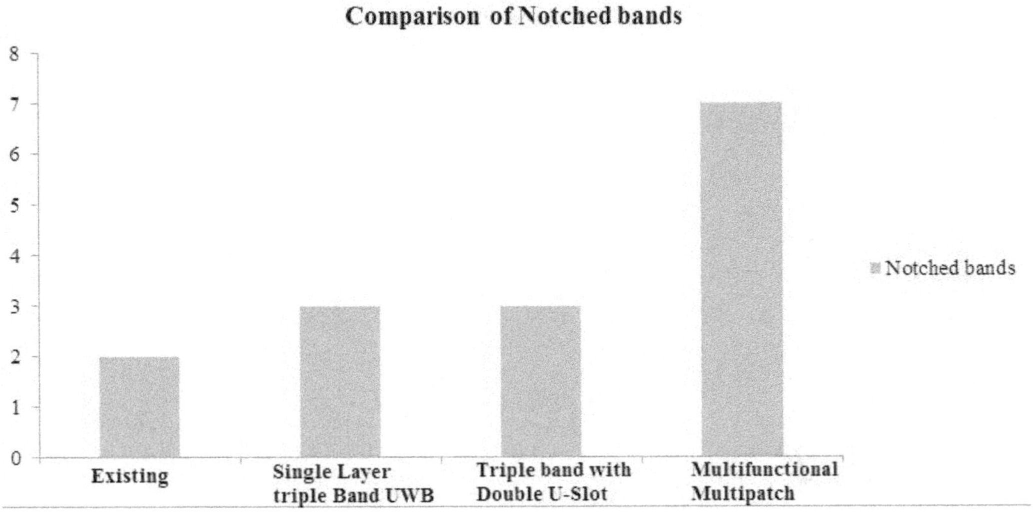

(a) Notched Bands

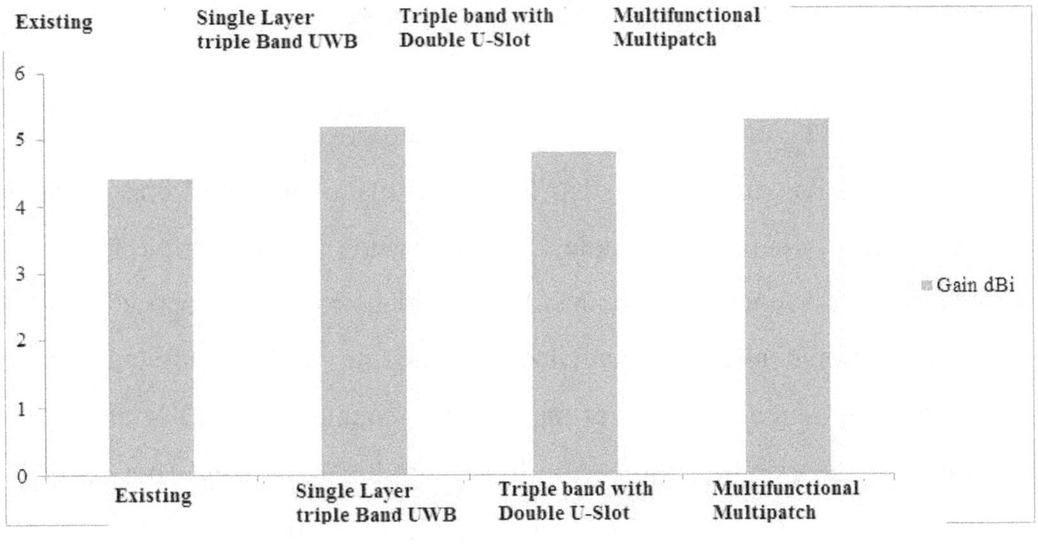

(b) Gain

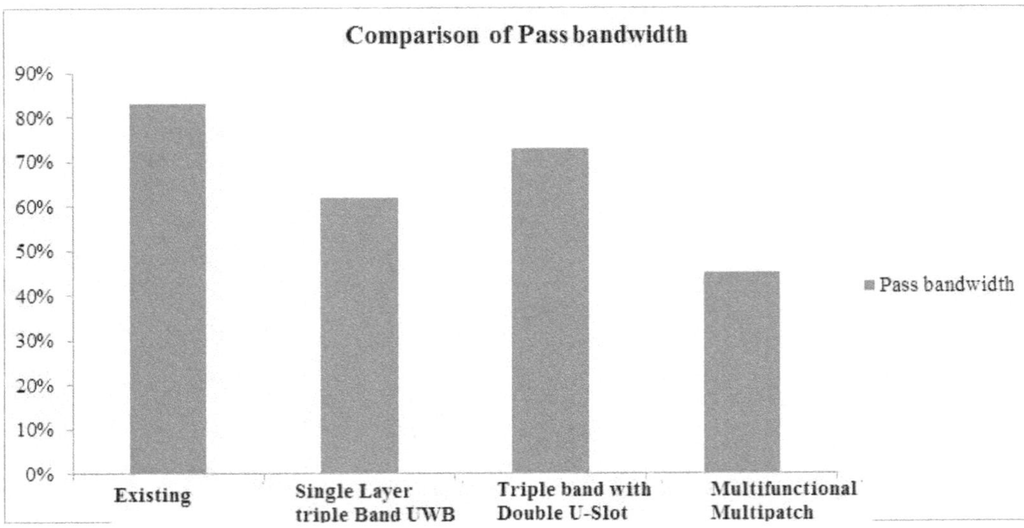

(c) Pass Bandwidth

Figure 7.1 Comparative Analyses of Notched Band Antenna Systems

Figure 7.1 (a) portrays the comparison of the number of notched bands. The conventional system has capability of notching only 2 bands of frequencies, whereas the single layer ultra-wide bandand triple band double layer systems notches three band of frequencies. The proposed multilayer multifunctional microstrip antenna with double U-slot exhibited 7 notched bands. The frequency bands of the existing scheme are 3.5 GHz and 5.5 GHz, whereas the single compact ultra-wide band antenna provided three frequencies as 3.5 GHz, 5.5 GHz and 8.2 GHz. The triple band with double U-slot antenna at 0.6 mm of the substrate resulted in 1.2 GHz, 2.2 GHz and 4.8 GHz frequencies, whereas the same at 1.6 mm substrate provided 1.5 GHz, 1.99 GHz and 3.8 GHz frequencies. The seven frequencies offered by the multifunctional multi patch microstrip antenna has been recorded as 1.5 GHz, 1.9 9 GHz, 2.23 GHz, 3 GHz, 3.5 GHz, 3.9 GHz and 4.9 GHz.

Figure 7.1 (b) depicts the comparative analysis of the gain of the systems taken up for study and the existing system. The gain of the existing system is found to be lower compared to the proposed systems. It offered a gain value of 4.4 dBi. The change in the design methodology of the various addressed schemes offered improvement in the gain. The gain of the single layer ultra-wide bandantenna has been found to higher than the existing antenna scheme and the triple band single layer with double U slot systems. The gain values have been observed as 5.2 dBi, 4.4 dBi and 4.8 dBi. It has been observed that the multifunctional multipatch antenna offered highest gain of 5.3 dBi. The gain value has been improved due to double U-slots and multifunctional multi patch approach.

Figure 7.1 (c) displays the evaluation of pass bandwidths of the existing and investigation schemes of interest. The existing system pass bandwidth is 83%, whereas the single layer ultra-wide bandantenna scheme offered 62%, the triple band with double U slot patch antenna resulted in 73%. The multifunctional multipatch antenna scheme the pass bandwidth is observed as 45%. This indicates that the multifunctional multipatch antenna scheme attenuates the unwanted frequencies to a greater extent compared to the other schemes taken up for study. This scheme is followed by the single layer ultra-wide band as it is capable of attenuating frequencies slightly lesser than multifunctional multipatch antenna. But the triple band notch antenna with double U slot and the existing schemes offered poor pass bandwidth.

The voltage standing wave ratio of all the schemes of interest taken up for study resulted in the similar gain of less than 2. All the proposed antenna arrangements and the existing antenna too had the same level of VSWR. These analyses exhibit the superiority of the multifunctional multipatch antenna with double U-slot provides better performance indices compared to its conventional and proposed counterparts.

7.2.2 Pass Band Antenna Systems

The comparative analysis of the existing antenna with the proposed compact CPW-fed microstrip antenna has been addressed in the section 6.7.1. The measured values of the proposed CPW-fed antenna, that has been tabulated in Table 6.2 and the corresponding analysis have been depicted in Figure 6.10 have been presented here for the reference.

Table 7.2 Comparative Analysis of existing and CPW-fed antenna scheme

Parameter	Existing Antenna	Proposed Antenna
Notched bands	2	3
Gain dBi	4.4	5.2
VSWR	<2	<2
Pass bandwidth %	60	81

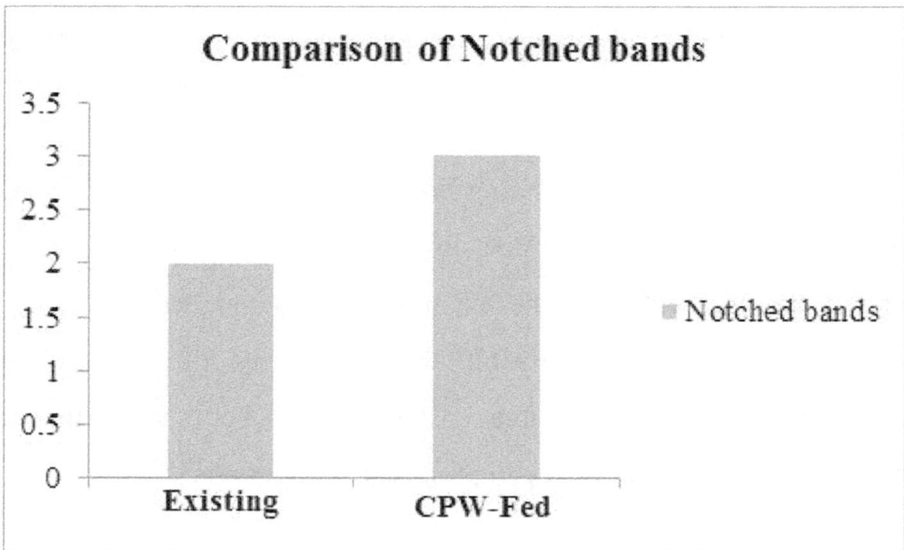

(a) Notched Bands

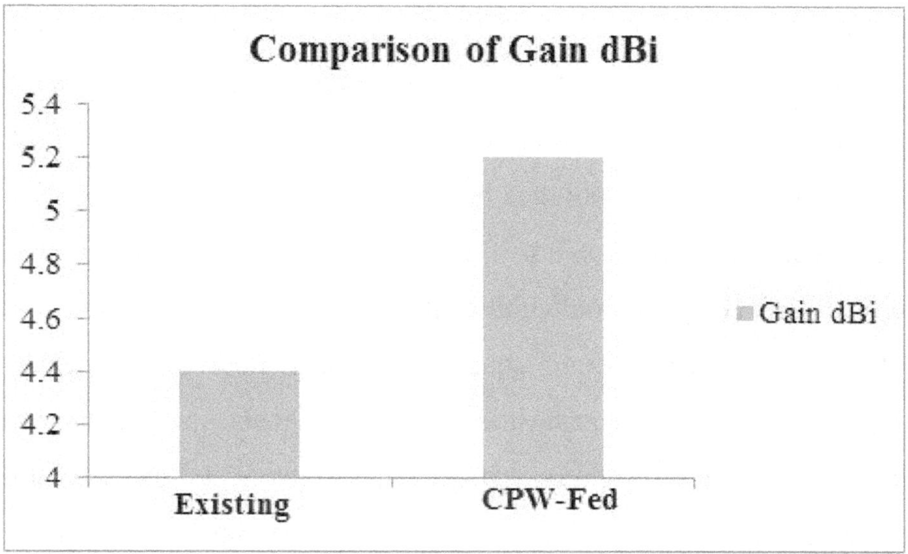

(b) Gain

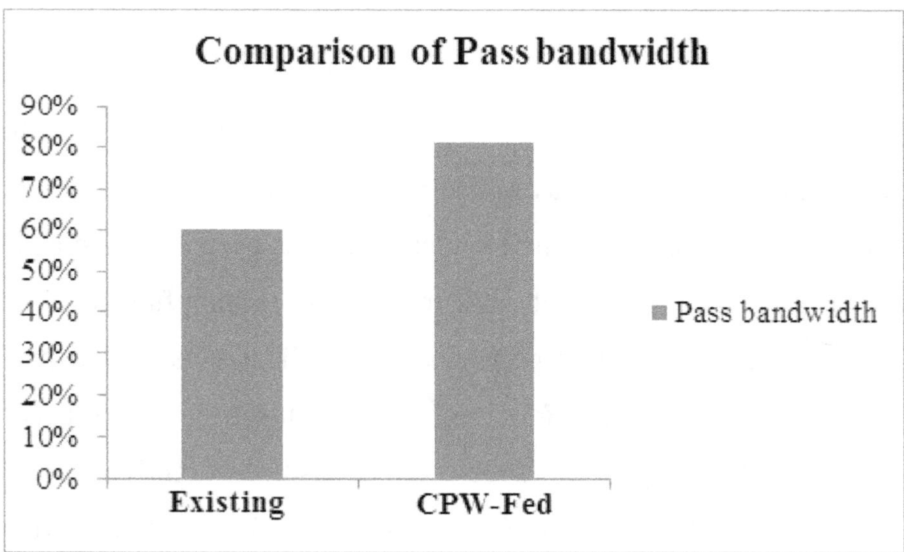

(c) Pass Bandwidth

Figure 7.2 Comparative Analyses of various antenna schemes

From the Table 6.2 and the corresponding analysis depicted in Figure 6.10 depicts that the proposed CPW-fed antenna provided 3 notched bands as 1.85 GHz, 3.50 GHz and 5.10 GHz for GSM, WiMAX and Wi-Fi applications. This is higher compared to the existing antenna scheme.

Enhanced gain also resulted in the CPW-fed antenna is higher as 5.2 dBi, whereas it is 4.4 dBi for the existing scheme. The reason for the same enhanced gain is due to the modifications made in the antenna structure. The voltage standing wave ratio has been found to be in line for both the systems. It has been observed as less than 2 for both the systems considered for comparison. The pass bandwidth of the proposed CPW-fed antenna scheme is 81%, whereas the existing scheme has only 60%. This means that the proposed scheme propagates the necessary signals up to 81% whereas the existing scheme propagation efficiency is only 60%. The existing scheme attenuates even the original signals. This problem has been suppressed by the CPW-fed proposed antenna scheme.

7.3 CONCLUSION

The performance analyses of the proposed schemes have been studied on two cases, one as notch band and another for the pass band. The results obtained from the experimental set up has been tabulated and analyzed for both the cases. The results illustrated that the multifunctional multipatch antenna exhibited superior performance on all aspects of the performance parameters. The scheme is followed by single layer ultra-wide band antenna. The results of the triple band double U-slot has been slightly higher compared to the existing scheme. The other case is the pass band antenna structure. The comparative analysis stated that the proposed CPW-fed antenna scheme provided better performance than the existing scheme. But when all the schemes of interest are taken into consideration, it is evident that the performance of the multifunctional multipatch antenna offers greater performance, as it offered 7 operating bands with a gain of 5.3 dBi. The VSWR is less than 2 and the pass bandwidth is 45%. These analyses make it clear that the proposed the multifunctional multipatch antenna can be effectively used for GSM, Wi-Fi, WiMAX and WLAN applications.

CHAPTER 8

CONCLUSION

8.1 SUMMARY AND CONTRIBUTIONS

The desired features expected by an antenna s the operating notched bands, voltage standing wave ratio, gain and the pass bandwidths. The existing antenna scheme offered poor performance parameters. The performance of the antenna scheme has to be improved such that, they found suitable for a wide range of frequency applications viz. GSM, Wi-MAX, Wi-Fi and WLAN systems. To have the desirable features cited above, certain improved antenna configurations have been proposed in this thesis. Among the configurations proposed the multifunctional multipatch antenna scheme exhibited superior quality. The main contributions of the thesis are summarized as follows:

- The objective of the thesis was to propose a suitable antenna scheme for wireless communication systems.
- An extensive study has been made on the existing research works addressed by various researchers.
- From the literature studies, it has been decided to propose a single layer microstrip fed ultra-wide bandantenna and to study its characteristics.

- In addition to it, the triple band notched antenna with double U-slot and multifunctional multipatch antenna schemes were also been considered.
- Finally, a compact CPW-fed antenna scheme was also studied.
- All the proposed antenna configurations have been modeled and simulated Using Ansoft HFSS version 13.0.
- The results of the simulation model viz. return loss, gain, and VSWR and radiation pattern in the H and E planes have been observed.
- The simulated results have to be validated through experimental set up, for which experimental designs have been proposed for all the antenna schemes of interest.
- The substrates of the experimental model have been devised using FR4 substrate with specific dielectric constant of 4.6 or less than that, with loss tangent as 0.02.
- The length and width of the designs have been optimized as per the frequency operating bands
- The results of the experimental model have been analyzed using Agilent's network analyzer.
- The results measured from the analyzer viz. return losses, voltage standing wave ratio and smith chart analyses have been portrayed.
- All the simulation and experimental results have been compared and analyzed.
- To validate the effectiveness of the proposed antenna configurations, a comparative analysis has been made on two aspects.
- One on the schemes of interest of notched bands and other on the pass bands.

- The results of the existing scheme are 2 notched bands, with gain of 4.4 dBi, VSWR < 2 and pass bandwidth of 83%.
- The proposed single layer ultra-wide bandantenna scheme offered 3 notched bands, with gain of 5.2 dBi, VSWR < 2 and pass bandwidth of 62%.
- The another scheme of interest that is triple layer with double U-slot provided 3 notched bands, with 4.8 dBi gain, VSWR < 2 and pass bandwidth of 7%.
- The attempted multifunctional multipatch antenna scheme resulted in superior performance indices compared to the other investigates antenna configurations.
- The results offered by the multifunctional multipatch antenna are 7 notched bands, gain 5.3 dBi, VSWR < 2 and pass bandwidth of 45%.
- For the pass band analysis, the existing scheme offered 60% pass bandwidth.
- The compact CPW-fed antenna scheme proposed for the pass band resulted in 3 notched bands, 5.2 dBi gain, and VSWR < 2 and pass bandwidth of 81%.
- The VSWR of all the investigated antenna configurations found to be less than 2.
- Form, all these results it can be concluded that the proposed multifunctional multipatch antenna scheme provides superior performance compared to its counterparts.
- These evidenced that the attempted multifunctional multipatch antenna scheme can be effectively utilized for wireless communication systems viz. GSM, Wi-Fi, Wi-MAX and WLAN applications.
- The objective of the research work is to improve the scalability and availability of the proposed 3 antenna schemes of interest. The

research has been focused and carried out to significantly improve the efficiency of the antenna schemes based on return loss, pass bandwidth and gain. By this way, the radiation pattern and polarization are enhanced. Hence, other parameters have not been considered.

8.2 SUGGESTIONS FOR FUTURE WORK

As the schemes analyzed in this thesis exhibit different values of return loss, pass bandwidth and gain, the reasons for them are due to the modifications in the antenna design viz. length, width and the substrate on which the antenna is devised. These design parameters can be optimized using any soft computing or evolutionary algorithms and the results may be discussed.

REFERENCES

1. Adam Narbudowicz; Matthias John ; Vit Sipal ; Xiulong Bao ; Max J. Ammann,2015,'Design Method for Wideband Circularly Polarized Slot Antennas,' IEEE Antennas and Propagation Letter, vol.63,no.10, pp. 4271- 4279.

2. Ahmed H. Khidre, Kai-Fong Lee,2013, 'Wide Band Dual-Beam U-Slot Microstrip Antenna', EEE Transactions on Antennas and Propagation, vol. 03, no.01,pp.45-56.

3. Ahmed T. M, Mohammad T. I and Rezaul. A,2013, 'Design Of A Dual Band-Notch Ultra-wide band (UWB) Slot Antenna By Means Of Simple Parasitic Slits', Microwave and Optical Technology Letters, vol. 16, no. 1, pp. 216-226.

4. Ahmed Toaha Mobashsher, Mohammad Tariqul Islam and Rezaul Azim, 2013 'Design of a Dual Band-Notch ultra-wide bandSlot Antenna by Means of Simple Parasitic Slits', IEEE Antennas and Wireless Propagation Letters,vol. 12, no.2, pp. 1412-1415.

5. Amin Araghi and Vorya Waladi,2015, 'Very Compact ultra-wide band Printed Monopole Antenna with Dual Band Notched Characteristics', International Journal of Natural and Engineering Sciences,vol. 7, no.3, pp. 82-86.

6. Araghi Amin and Waladi Vorya,2013 , 'Very compact ultra-wide band printed monopole antenna with dual band notched characteristics', International Journal of Natural & Engineering Sciences, vol.7, no.3, pp. 82-86.

7. Aykut Cihangir, Fabien Ferrero,Gilles Jacquemod,2014 'Neutralized Coupling Elements for MIMO Operation in 4G Mobile Terminals', IEEE Antennas and Propagation Magazine,vol.13,no.1,pp. 2134-2144.

8. AnilkrGautam, Aykut Cihangir, Fabien Ferrero,Gilles Jacquemod,2014, 'Neutralized Coupling Elements for MIMO Operation in 4G Mobile Terminals', IEEE Antennas and Propagation Magazine,vol.13, pp. 22-26.

9. Bin Xu, et.al.,2013,'A CPW-fed dual band-notched ultra-wide band antenna with a pair of bended dual-L-shape parasitic branches', Progress in Electromagnetics Research,vol. 136,no.8, pp. 623-634.

10. Bo Li, et.al.,2012,'A dual band-notched ultra-wide bandprinted antenna with C-shaped and a U-shaped slot', Microwave and Optical Technology Letters, vol.54, no.6, pp. 1450-1452.

11. Chao-Tang Chuang and Shyh-Jong Chung, 2011, 'Synthesis and design of a new printed filtering antenna', IEEE Transactions on Antennas and Propagation, vol.59, no.4, pp. 1036–1042.

12. Chen W. S. and Yu, Y. H.2008, 'Compact design of T-type monopole antenna with asymmetrical ground plane for WLAN/WiMAX applications', Microwave Optical Technology Letter, vol. 50, no. 2, pp. 515–519.

13. Chen Wang, et.al., (2012), 'A Dual Band-Notched Ultra-wide band (UWB) Printed Antenna With C-Shaped And A U-Shaped Slot', IEEE Transactions on Antennas and Propagation, vol.56, no.2, pp. 356–367

14. Cheung. S. W, Weng. Y. F and Yuk. T. I, (2010), 'Triple Band-Notched Ultra-wide band (UWB) Antenna Using Meandered Ground Stubs', IEEE Antennas and Wireless Propagation Letters, vol. 8, no. 2, pp. 87-92.

15. Cheung. S. W, Weng. Y. F and Yuk. T. I, 2010,'Triple Band-Notched ultra-wide bandAntenna using Meandered Ground Stubs', Antennas & Propagation Conference, vol. 8, no. 22, pp. 341-344.

16. Costantine, J. Kabalan, K. Y. El-Hajj, A. and Rammal, M.2007,'New multiband microstrip antenna design for wireless communications',IEEE Transaction Antennas Propagation Magazine, vol. 49, no. 6, pp. 181–186.

17. Damir Zayniyev and Djuradj Budimir, 2010, 'Dual-band microstrip antenna filter for wireless communications', Proceedings of the IEEE Antennas and Propagation Society International Symposium.pp.567-577.

18. Dan Feng ; Huiqing Zhai ; Lei Xi ; Sen Yang ; Kedi Zhang ; Dong Yang,2017, 'A Broadband Low-Profile Circular-Polarized Antenna on an AMC Reflector', IEEE Antennas and Wireless Propagation Letters,vol.16,no1,pp. 2840- 2843.

19. Dang Trang Nguyen ; Dong Hyun Lee ; Hyun Chang Park,2012,'Very Compact Printed Triple Band-Notched ultra-wide bandAntenna With Quarter-Wavelength Slots',IEEE Antennas and Wireless Propagation Letters,vol. 11,no.2.pp. 411-414.

20. Eugean Kim ; Seung-Tae Ko; Young Ju Lee;2018 'A Broadband Low-Profile Circular-Polarized Antenna on an AMC Reflector', IEEE Antennas and Wireless Propagation Letters,vol.15,no.5,pp. 845 - 848.

21. Fan Yang, 2003, 'Microstrip Antennas Integrated With Electromagnetic Band-Gap (EBG) Structures: A Low Mutual Coupling Design for Array Applications' , IEEE Antennas and Propagation Magazine,vol.51,no.10,pp-45-56.

22. Hassan Tariq Chattha, Ping Cao and Yi Huang,2011,'Reducing Ground-Plane Effects on ultra-wide bandMonopole Antennas', IEEE Antennas and Wireless Propagation Letters, vol. 10,no.3,pp. 147-150.

23. Hattan F. AbuTarboush; R. Nilavalan ; Thomas Peter ; S. W. Cheung,2011, 'Multiband Inverted-F Antenna With Independent Bands for Small and Slim Cellular Mobile Handsets',IEEE Transaction Antennas Propagation Magazine, Vol. 59, no. 7, pp. 2636 - 2645.

24. Hong Chen, Yang, X. Yin, Y. Z. Fan, S. T. and Wu J. J.2013,'Triband Planar Monopole Antenna With Compact Radiator for WLAN/WiMAX Applications', IEEE Antennas And Wireless Propagation Letters, vol. 12,no.3,pp. 1440-1443.

25. Hong-wei Deng ; Tao Xu ; Fei Liu,2018, 'Broadband Pattern-Reconfigurable Filtering Microstrip Antenna With Quasi-Yagi Structure', IEEE Antennas and Wireless Propagation Letters,vol.17,no.7, pp. 1127- 1131.

26. Horng-Dean Chen; Chow-Yen-Desmond Sim ; Shang-Huang Kuo,2012, 'Compact Broadband Dual Coupling-Feed Circularly Polarized RFID Microstrip Tag Antenna Mountable on Metallic Surface', IEEE Antennas and Wireless Propagation Letters, vol.60.no.12,pp. 5571-5577.

27. Hsi-Tseng Chou;Yao-Jiu Chen;Hsien-Kwei Ho,2018, 'An All-Metallic Reflectarray and Its Element Design: Exploring the Radiation Characteristics of Antennas for Directional Beam Applications', IEEE Antennas and Propagation Magazine, vol.60,no.05,pp. 41-51.

28. Hui Li ; Le Kang ; Feng Wei ; Yuan-Ming Cai ; Ying-Zeng Yin,2017 "A Low-Profile Dual-Polarized Microstrip Antenna Array for Dual-Mode OAM Applications",IEEE Antennas and Wireless Propagation Letters, vol.16, pp. 3022-3025.

29. Huynh T and K.-F. Lee,1995, 'Single-layer single-patch wideband microstrip antenna', IET Digital Library, vol.31, no.16,pp.234-244.

30. Haroon S, K.-S. Alimgeer, N. Khalid, B.-T. Malik, M.-F. Shafique, and S.-A. Khan,2014,'A Low Profile ultra-wide bandAntenna with Triple Band Suppression Characteristics' ,Wireless Pers. Commun., vol. 10, pp. 100-112.

31. Jesús Rubio ; Juan F. Izquierdo,2011,'Relation Between the Array Pattern Approach in Terms of Coupling Coefficients and Minimum Scattering Antennas', IEEE Transaction Antennas Propagation Magazine,vol.59, no.7, pp. 2532 – 2537.

32. Jiao-Jiao Xie, et.al.,2011'A New Compact Filter-Antenna for Modern Wireless Communication Systems', IEEE Antennas and Wireless Propagation Letters, nol. 10, no.10, pp. 1131-1134.

33. Jingli Guo,Yanlin Zou,Chao Li,2011, 'Compact Broadband Crescent Moon-Shape Patch-Pair Antenna' IEEE Antennas and wave propagation letter,vol.10, no.04,pp. 1356-1365.

34. Junhui-H. Wang, Xianglong-L. Liu and Yingzeng-Z. Yin,2013, 'A Compact Dual Band-Notched Ultra-wide band (UWB) Antenna With Meandering Slot And C-Shape Strips', IEEE Antennas and Wireless Propagation Letters, vol. 6, no. 12, pp.2752-2763.

35. Junhui-H. Wang,Xianglong-L. Liu and Yingzeng-Z. Yin, 2013,'A Compact Dual band-notched ultra-wide bandantenna with Meandering slot and C-shape strips', Microwave and Optical Technology Letters,vol. 55, no.11, pp. 2631-2636.

36. Ka Ming Mak; Hua Wah Lai; Kwai Man Luk,2018,'A 5G Wideband Patch Antenna With Antisymmetric L-shaped Probe Feeds,' IEEE Transactions on Antennas and Propagation, Vol.66,no.2, pp. 957-961.

37. Kevin Ming-Jiang Ho ; Gabriel M. Rebeiz,2014,'A 0.9–1.5 GHz Microstrip Antenna With Full Polarization Diversity and Frequency Agility',IEEE Antennas and Wireless Propagation Letters,vol. 62,no.5, pp. 2398 - 2406.

38. Le Kang, Hui Li, Xinhuai Wang,2015, 'Compact Offset Microstrip-Fed MIMO Antenna for Band-Notched ultra-wide bandApplications',IEEE Antennas and Wireless Propagation Letters, 2015 vol.14,no.pp. 1754 - 1757.

39. Lee K. F., et. Al.,2012, 'On The Use Of U-Slots In The Design Of Dual- And Triple-Band Patch Antennas', IEEE Antennas and Propagation Magazine, vol.53, no.03 , pp. 60-74.

40. Lee K. F., et.al.,2010, 'The Versatile U-Slot Patch Antenna', IEEE Antennas and Propagation Magazine, vol.52,no.01,pp. 71-88.

41. Lev Pazin ; Yehuda Leviatan,2014,'Reconfigurable Rotated-T Slot Antenna for Cognitive Radio Systems', IEEE Antennas and Wireless Propagation Letters, vol.62,no.5, pp. 2382-2387.

42. Li Ying Feng;Kwok Wa Leung,2016,'Dual-Frequency Folded-Parallel-Plate Antenna With Large Frequency Ratio', IEEE Antennas and Propagation Letter, vol.64, no.1, pp. 340–345.

43. Liu W. C,2013, 'Design of a multiband CPW-fed monopole antenna using a particle swarm optimization approach', IEEE Transaction of Antennas Propagation, vol. 53, no. 10, pp. 3273–3279.

44. Mallikarjuna P., Naresh K. D., and Ramana R. R.,2015, 'Design Of Triple-Layer Double U-Slot Patch Antenna For Wireless Applications', Journal of applied research and technology, vol.13, no.05,pp.567-577.

45. Mohamad Yazdi and Nader Komjani,2013 'Planar ultra-wide band monopole antenna with dual band-notched characteristics for ultra-wide band applications', Microwave Optical Technology Letters, vol.55,no.2,pp. 241–245.

46. Mohamed Tarbouch ; Abdelkebir El Amri ; Hanae Terchoune,2017, 'Compact CPW-Fed microstrip octagonal patch antenna with H slot for WLAN and WIMAX applications' IEEE Transactions on Antennas and Propagation,vol. 65,no.12, pp. 6231 - 6249.

47. Mohamed Tarbouch; Abdelkebir El Amri; Hanae Terchoune, 2017,'Compact CPW-Fed microstrip octagonal patch antenna with H slot for WLAN and WIMAX applications,' IEEE Antennas and Wireless Propagation Letters, vol. 12,no.2,pp. 151-154.

48. Mu'ath J. Al-Hasan, Tayeb A. Denidni, and Abdel Razik Sebak,2011, 'Millimeter-wave Compact EBG Structure for Mutual Coupling Reduction Applications', IEEE Antennas and Propagation Magazine, vol.10,pp.134-147.

49. Naser Ojaroudiparchin, Ming Shen, Shuai Zhang,2016, 'A Switchable 3-D-Coverage-Phased Array Antenna Package for 5G Mobile Terminals', IEEE Antennas and Wireless Propagation Letters, vol.15,no.1,pp. 1747 - 1750.

50. Naser-Moghadasi, M. Sadeghzadeh, R. Asadpor, L. and Virdee, B. S.2013, 'A Small Dual-Band CPW-Fed Monopole Antenna for GSM and WLAN Applications', IEEE Antennas and Wireless propagation letters,vol. 12,no.2, pp. 508-511.

51. Nasimuddin N ,Zhi Ning Chen ; Xianming Qing,2016, 'Bandwidth Enhancement of a Single-Feed Circularly Polarized Antenna Using a

Metasurface: Metamaterial-based wideband CP rectangular microstrip antenna', IEEE Antennas and Propagation Magazine, vol.58, no.02.

52. Neng-Wu Liu ; Lei Zhu ; Wai-Wa Choi ; Jin-Dong Zhang, 2018, 'A Low-Profile Differentially Fed Microstrip Patch Antenna With Broad Impedance Bandwidth Under Triple-Mode Resonance', IEEE Antennas and Wireless Propagation Letters,vol.17, no.8,pp. 1478-1482.

53. Ojaroudi and Ebarhimian,2012, 'A dual band-notched ultra-wide bandprinted antenna with C-shaped and U-shaped slots', Microwave Optical Technology Letters, vol.54, no.6, pp. 1450–1452.

54. Patnam H. Rao Sathiyamoorthy Sujitha ; Krishnasamy T. Selvan,2017, 'A Multiband, Mutipolarization Shared-Aperture Antenna: Design and evaluation', IEEE Antennas and Propagation Magazine, vol.59, no.04, pp. 26-37.

55. Peng Fei ,Yong-Chang Jiao ; Wei Hu,2010, 'A compact CPW-fed finger-shaped antenna for ultra-wide bandapplication',IEEE Proceedings of the 9th International Symposium on Antennas, Propagation and EM Theory.

56. Ping Wang, Guang-Jun Wen, Yong-Jun Huang and Yuan-Hua Sun,2012, 'Compact CPW-fed planar monopole antenna with distinct triple bands for WiFi/WiMAX applications', Electronics Letters,vol. 48, no.7,pp.23-34.

57. Pingan Liu, Yanlin Zou, Baorong Xie, Xianglong Liu, and Baohua Sun,2012, 'Compact CPW-Fed Tri-Band Printed Antenna With Meandering Split-Ring Slot for WLAN/WiMAX Applications', IEEE Antennas and Wireless Propagation Letters, Vol. 11, no.2,pp. 1242-1244.

58. Qing-Xin Chu and Ying-Ying Yang,2008, 'A compact ultra wide band antenna with 3.4/5.5 GHz dual band-notched characteristics' , IEEE Transactions onAntennas and Propagation, vol. 56, no.12, pp. 3637–3644.

59. Rezaul Azim, Mohammad Tariqul Islam and Ahmed Toaha Mobashsher, 2013, 'Design of a dual band-notch ultra-wide band slot antenna by means of simple parasitic slits' IEEE Antennas and Wireless Propagation Letters, vol.12, no.8, pp. 1412–1415.

60. Rezaul Azim, Mohammad Tariqul Islam and Ahmed Toaha Mobashsher,2014'Dual band-notch ultra-wide bandantenna with single tri-arm resonator', IEEE Antennas and Wireless Propagation Letters,vol.13,no.8,pp. 670-673.

61. Ruina Lian, Zedong Wang, Yingzeng Yin,2015, 'Design of a Low-Profile Dual-Polarized Stepped Slot Antenna Array for Base Station', IEEE Antennas and Wireless Propagation Letters,vol.15, no.8, pp. 362 - 365.

62. Ruina Lian, Zedong Wang, Yingzeng Yin,2016, 'Design of a Low-Profile Dual-Polarized Stepped Slot Antenna Array for Base Station',IEEE Antennas and Wireless Propagation Letters,vol.14, no.3,pp. 362 - 365.

63. Sabita Yadav, K K Saini, 2015, 'Case Study of WiMAX Technology & Its Application With Respect to Microstrip Patch Antenna,' Microw. Opt. Technol. Letter,vol.06,no.3,pp. 747–749.

64. Sai Hoi Wong,Sing V K et.al.2013, 'Single-Layer Single-Patch Dual-Band And Triple-Band Patch Antennas', International Journal of Advances in Electrical and Electronics Engineering, vol.03,no.01,pp. 1445-1455.

65. Samavia Haroon, Khurram Saleem Alimgeer, Nihala Khalid, Bilal Tariq Malik, Farhan Shafique and Shahid Khan,2014, 'A low profile ultra-wide bandantenna with triple band suppression characteristics' , Wireless Personal Communications, vol.10, no.1, pp. 100-11.

66. Tero Uusitupa ; Takahiro Aoyagi,2013,'Analysis of Dynamic On-Body Communication Channels for Various Movements and Polarization Schemes at 2.45 GHz', IEEE Antennas and Wireless Propagation Letters,vol.61,no 12,pp. 6168 – 6179.

67. Umair Naeem, Stéphane Bila, Serge Verdeyme, Marc Thévenot and Thierry Monédière,2010, 'A compact dual band filter-antenna subsystem for 802.11 Wi-Fi applications' , Proceeding of the 3rd European Wireless Technology Conference, Pages 181-184.

68. Wei-Jun Wu, Ying-Zeng Yin and Shao-Li Zuo,2011, 'A new compact filter-antenna for modern wireless communication systems' , IEEE Antennas and Wireless Propagation Letters, vol.10, no.10, pp. 1131-1134.

69. Wen Jiang and Wenquan Che,2012 'A novel ultra-wide bandantenna with dual notched bands for WiMAX and WLAN applications', IEEE Antennas and Wireless Propagation Letters, vol. 11, no.7,pp. 293-296.

70. Wen Jiang and WenquanChe. (2012), 'A Novel ultra-wide bandAntenna With Dual Notched Bands for WiMAX and WLAN Applications', IEEE Antennas and Wireless Propagation Letters, vol. 11,no.5pp. 293–296.

71. Wenxing An ; Xu Wang ; Haipeng Fu ; Jianguo Ma ; Xiangdong Huang ; Botao Feng,2018, 'Low-Profile Wideband Slot-Loaded Patch Antenna With Multiresonant Modes',IEEE Antennas and Wireless Propagation Letters, vol.17,no.7,pp. 1309- 1313.

72. Wu, C. M. Chiu, C. N. and Hsu, C. K.,2006,'A new non-uniform meandered and fork-type grounded antenna for triple-band WLAN applications', IEEE Antennas Wireless Propagation Letter, vol. 5,no.1pp. 346–348.

73. Xianglong Liu, Yingzeng Yin, Pingan Liu, Junhui Wang and Bin Xu,2013 , 'A CPW-fed dual band-notched ultra-wide bandantenna with a pair of bended dual-l-shape parasitic branches' , Progress In Electromagnetics Research, vol.136,no.7, pp. 623–634.

74. Xianglong-L.Liu, Yingzeng-Z.Yin and Junhui-H.Wang,2013'A compact dual band-notched ultra-wide bandantenna with meandering slot and C-shape strips', Microwave and Optical Technology Letters, vol.55, no.11, pp. 2631–2636.

75. Xiaodi, S.2009, 'Small CPW-fed triple band microstrip monopole antenna for WLAN applications,' Microwave Optical Technology Letter,vol. 51, no. 3, pp. 747–749.

76. Xu, Y. Jiao, Y.-C and Luan Y.-C.2012,'Compact CPW-fed printed monopole antenna with triple-band characteristics for WLAN/WiMAX applications', Electronics Letters, vol. 48 no. 24,pp.90-99.

77. XueMing Ling and RongLin Li,2011, 'A Novel Dual-Band MIMO Antenna ArrayWith Low Mutual Coupling for Portable Wireless Devices',IEEE Antennas and Propagation Magazine, vol.10,no.7, pp. 658-667.

78. Yang Lu, Yi Huang and Hassan Tariq Chattha,2011,'Reducing ground-plane effects on ultra-wide bandmonopole antennas', IEEE Antennas and Wireless Propagation Letters, vol. 10, no.3, pp. 147–150.

79. Yun-Jui Lee, Gang-Wei Cao and Shyh-Jong Chung, 2012, 'A compact dual-band filtering microstrip antenna with the same polarization planes', Asia Pacific Microwave Conference Proceedings, pp. 1178-1180.

www.ingramcontent.com/pod-product-compliance
Lightning Source LLC
LaVergne TN
LVHW082340200926
848481LV00012B/3401
* 9 7 9 8 2 3 2 2 0 6 9 1 8 *